GEORGE BARNA

MARKETING THE CHURCH

NAVPRESS

A MINISTRY OF THE NAVIGATORS
P.O. BOX 35001, COLORADO SPRINGS, COLORADO 80935

The Navigators is an international Christian organization. Jesus Christ gave His followers the Great Commission to go and make disciples (Matthew 28:19). The aim of The Navigators is to help fulfill that commission by multiplying laborers for Christ in every nation.

NavPress is the publishing ministry of The Navigators. NavPress publications are tools to help Christians grow. Although publications alone cannot make disciples or change lives, they can help believers learn biblical discipleship, and apply what they learn to their lives and ministries.

Library of Congress Catalog Card Number: 88-60625
ISBN 08910-92501

Eighth printing, 1992

Cover illustration: Jeff Lauwers

Scripture quotations in this publication are from the *Holy Bible: New International Version* (NIV). Copyright © 1973, 1978, 1984, International Bible Society. Used by permission of Zondervan Bible Publishers.

Printed in the United States of America

Contents

104209

Author

George Barna is the president of the Barna Research Group, a full-service marketing research company located in Glendale, California. After graduating summa cum laude from Boston College, George earned two masters degrees from Rutgers University. At Rutgers, he was awarded an Eagleton Fellowship. He began Barna Research in 1984.

In addition to *Marketing the Church*, George wrote *Vital Signs* (Crossway, 1984). He is the author of more than three dozen published articles, and is the publisher of *Christian Marketing Perspective*, a quarterly newsletter about trends affecting the Christian community.

Currently a faculty member at Biola University, Barna lives with his wife, Nancy, in Glendale, California.

Acknowledgments

No nonfiction book of any substance can be written without considerable influence from individuals who have been a part of the author's life. We are all products of our environment, and the environmental element that shapes our thoughts and experiences most dramatically is the other human beings we encounter. Like every author, my work is a blend of personal experiences, formal education, and interaction with a variety of wise and generous individuals.

I am indebted to Bill Hybels, pastor of Willow Creek Community Church near Chicago, for his vision and relentless quest to see that vision become a reality for the glory of God. It was during my time in Wheaton, Illinois, while attending Rev. Hybels' church, that I first had my eyes opened to the meaning of evangelism and church growth. If I had my way, there would be 100,000 Willow Creek Churches in this country. With God's blessing, perhaps we can make some headway toward that goal.

I am grateful to many pastors, lay leaders, marketing professionals, and colleagues who have taken the time and care to read earlier drafts of this manuscript and to provide invaluable insight into how to share my ideas more effectively. Among those who especially deserve my thanks are my colleague in business and ministry, Rob Michaels, and my friend and spiritual mentor, Bill Tibert.

I would also be remiss if I did not acknowledge the sacrifices made by my staff and colleagues at Barna Research Group. Hopefully absence makes the heart grow fonder, and as a result of having been an absentee leader while writing this book, my return to the daily duties of conducting our research will find me in my cohorts' favor. My special thanks go to Billie Gaughan, Ron Sellers, and Becky Temple for their patience and reliability.

It has been a pleasure to work with my editor at NavPress, Kathy Yanni. Kathy has demonstrated a sincerity about this work that has been challenging, and a patience with me that has been appreciated. Her encouragement at various steps along the way, not to mention her on-target and constructive criticism of my work, have been significant.

The most important person in this entire project has been my wife, Nancy. Through it all she has been there to inspire and challenge me, to comfort and humble me. Who else would agree to be subjected to endless drafts of chapters, some of which will never see the light of day? Nancy has been wholly supportive throughout this project and had a critical part in shaping the book. Without her as my partner in life and in ministry, I cannot imagine this book having come to pass. I pray that she will see the fruits of her sacrifices emerge from this book's impact on churches.

Finally, I offer this book, with many prayers, as a gift to

Jesus Christ, my Lord and Savior. It is His Church I seek to assist, sharing my ideas and experiences for the glory and expansion of His everlasting Kingdom.

INTRODUCTION
Church Growth: A Perspective You Won't Get in Seminary

Because of the business I'm in—I own a marketing research company that serves numerous Christian and secular organizations—I have the chance to speak at many conferences and seminars on church growth and development. As a result of my interaction with pastors and lay leaders, it seemed sensible to write a book that presented many of the principles offered in my seminars—principles that many of my clients have implemented for great gain.

After a contract had been hammered out, the publisher and I decided that the book would be published under its current title. Swept by the urge to practice what I preach, I began to promote the book months before its publication. Like an expectant father, I was anxious to learn more about people's perceptions of the product to which I would give birth.

Ironically, one insight I quickly picked up was that the

title of the book would present an interesting marketing problem. After telling pastors the title of the book, I typically received one of four responses:

- *Polite perplexity.* These kindly souls did a silent double take, with the brow furrowed and the head slightly cocked, as if I had suggested that Ronald Reagan was a communist.
- *Verbalized astonishment.* "It's called *what?*"
- *Spiritual challenge.* "Marketing, eh? Are you a Christian, Mr. Barna?"
- *Genuine enthusiasm.* "That's great. Tell me about it."

Let's be honest. The last reaction has been the least common. After all, anyone who speaks openly about marketing any facet of Christianity is likely to be branded "radical," if not downright "heretical."

The Problem of Marketing the Church
The Christian Church is not exactly known for setting trends or embracing change. Although marketing has been an accepted discipline in the business world for several decades, many Christian leaders consider even speaking of marketing a church as the next best thing to blasphemy.

And yet, I believe that developing a marketing orientation is precisely what the Church needs to do if we are to make a difference in the spiritual health of this nation for the remainder of this century.

This book presents a new way of thinking for those of us who are involved in local church leadership. It is not about a new way of perceiving the Lord Jesus Christ. He was, is, and forever will be the same loving, unique Savior that Scripture so clearly describes. The Bible's teaching about the unchanging nature of God is not to be doubted.

The new way of thinking I describe in this book pertains to how we can more effectively reach people with the good news about Christ's redemption. Some people in the Christian community refer to the types of activities I will address as *church growth strategies, bridge building,* or simply *church outreach and promotion.* However, I call these activities marketing.

It is no secret that we live in a world that is changing more rapidly and more dramatically than ever before. This is truly an era in which the expression "survival of the fittest" has meaning. If you study the American organizations that are thriving—whether you look at business, individuals, schools, even churches—they are characterized by the ability to adapt to change quickly and efficiently. Yet they do so without shedding their distinctive nature or sense of purpose.

For instance, look at Apple, the computer manufacturer. Initially, the company believed that its pathway to success was through selling computers to individuals for home use. The Apple IIe model was a wild success, and seemed to vindicate the plans of Apple's leaders. However, as the economy and people's perceptions of computers changed, so did Apple's ability to sell its systems to households. Accordingly, they shifted their emphasis to the educational and business markets. Apple maintained its identity and its unique sense of purpose, but changed its systems to allow the company to reach its goals. Apple adapted quickly and successfully to a changing environment and new attitudes.

Why We Have the Problem
I shared the early drafts of this book with some colleagues in the business world. One of their reactions was to question why a book describing basic marketing principles and applying them to the church would be seen as a novel idea or generate any interest.

The answer is simple. Consider the background of the average pastor. He graduates from college with a degree in religious studies or liberal arts. He enters seminary. In seminary he receives training in preaching, counseling, teaching, music, etc. He graduates and is called to ministry by a church. If the church is small, he may be the only minister on the payroll. If it is a medium-sized or large church, he might be one of several paid, full-time clergymen on the staff. After a while, he might ascend to the position of senior pastor at that or another good-sized church.

The average pastor has been trained in religious matters. Yet, upon assuming church leadership, he is asked to run a business! Granted, that business is a not-for-profit organization, but it is still a business. The Church is in the business of ministry: searching out people who need the gift of acceptance, forgiveness, and eternal life that is available in knowing Jesus Christ. For the local church to be a successful business, it must impact a growing share of its market area.

Ultimately, many people do judge the pastor not on his ability to preach, teach, or counsel, but on his capacity to make the church run smoothly and efficiently. In essence, he is judged as a businessman, an area in which he has received no training or preparation. In fact, even the pastor's ability to use his training in religious matters hinges on his business capabilities. He must be a good enough businessman to keep the church solvent and make it appealing enough for people to attend before he has the chance to impact their lives.

Some churches attempt to solve the problem of inadequate pastoral business preparation by calling on the expertise of lay leaders within the church. The Board of Elders, the Deacons, Trustees—depending on the denomination—is generally a committee designed to help manage the church's affairs.

However, the hard truth of the matter is that the people on

those committees, despite their best intentions and effort, generally are no better at making things happen for the church than the pastor. Why? Relatively few people actively involved in church leadership have the mix of business acumen and spiritual vision that would enable them to lead the church. Often those who have such ability lack either the commitment to the church or the required time to devote to church matters. In other situations, sharp businessmen in the church lack the necessary sensitivity to ministry.

Certainly there are alternatives to leadership by committee. The use of outside consultants is a possibility—if the church can raise the money to cover the consulting fees. Some church leaders do not even consider this option because they believe an outsider cannot have the required degree of sensitivity to the church's needs. Others fear that reliance on outside leadership will cripple the church by making it dependent on external assistance, thereby preventing the development of new leadership within the body.

Turning to the denomination for assistance is sometimes an option. Unfortunately, when it comes to church growth, many denominations have little to offer beyond words of encouragement. Others have specialists who approach church development from a macro perspective, rather than the micro approach a local church needs. Such specialists can provide a global understanding of church growth techniques, but are unable to translate those into the practical steps that a church needs.

In the end, many pastors learn that responsibility for operating the church comes back to the old Harry Truman philosophy: "The buck stops here." If the pastor wants to have something done right, he must often do it himself—or at least see that it is done right by others who have a heart to help the church.

This book is my attempt to help pastors and lay leaders

who are open to a new approach build an effective church. This book is not meant to be a substitute for an M.B.A. in marketing. However, it is designed to provide the first step toward helping church leaders think through what the business of ministry is all about and how the discipline of marketing fits into the calling of ministry.

A Response to the Skeptics

In listening to the reactions of leaders who have seen early versions of this book, and in answering questions raised at seminars and conferences, I have found four main concerns about the concept of marketing the church.

Marketing does not seem like a biblical practice.

Actually, the issue here is semantics. As I hope to show in the first section of this book, the Bible contains many instances of marketing, although we traditionally have not called those activities marketing. I pray that the mere words I use to communicate my perspective on church growth and development do not get in the way of the process. If you cannot get past the word *marketing,* try substituting words with which you are more comfortable, such as *outreach* or *development.*

Think about your experience for a minute. When you share your faith with a nonbeliever, you are actually marketing the church. When you place an advertisement in the newspaper to inform people of your church services, you are marketing your church. If your church has a sign on the church grounds, identifying the times of services, Sunday school classes, or even the title of the upcoming sermon, you are engaging in marketing. Every time your pastor accepts an invitation to offer a benediction at a public gathering (although he has been invited for the purpose of ministry), his presence and performance represent an exercise in marketing.

Perhaps more than you realize, your church is already involved in marketing, although we rarely call those actions marketing. Please don't ignore what I have to say simply because you feel uneasy with the term.

Church growth approaches are invariably insensitive to true ministry because they concentrate on numbers—building a large church. There's nothing wrong with a small church.

I wholeheartedly agree with people who raise this concern. In society today we are turned on by numbers—big numbers. The bigger, the better, we often reason. I am particularly aware of this mind-set because of my business—providing statistical reports and analyses to corporations whose success is judged according to how big the numbers are and how much the numbers have grown from one point in time to the next.

When it comes to churches, though, I believe God wants quality, not just quantity. Oh, certainly, He is interested in seeing every person develop a personal relationship with Jesus Christ and grow in that relationship through the help of the local church. Reaching all people is a part of our mission as God's people, but we also know that He despises lukewarm Christians (Matthew 7:21-27). Any church growth strategy that is geared to increasing the number of people without emphasizing the necessity of commitment to Jesus Christ is working in opposition to scriptural command.

Having said that, though, let me offer an observation. I believe there is an indivisible relationship between quality and quantity when it comes to church growth. In the early stages of a church's life cycle, new people are attracted to a church because it meets their personal needs. The more successful a church is at fulfilling people's needs, the greater are its chances for growth. Thus, quantity is a consequence of quality. Similarly, a church that has a quality ministry, but does not grow, may simply be suffering from inept marketing.

You can't tell me how to make my church grow. You don't understand the dynamics of our culture or our distinctives.

Sometimes that may be the case. Nobody will understand

the opportunities and obstacles for church growth better than the pastor and other church leaders. Allowing any external force—a person, a program, a structure, a system—to control your church and reshape its identity, without your direction and approval, would be sheer folly. But I am not recommending a rigid structure or series of rules and regulations. I am advocating a way of understanding your environment and responding to it. John Sculley, former president of PepsiCo, and current CEO (chief executive officer) of Apple, describes the marketing approach I am outlining as "less a single-minded discipline or set of skills than it is an attitude, *a way of thinking.*"[1]

Successful marketing requires an attitude of flexibility and adaptability. There is no single, right way to market a church. Every church is different and must pay special attention to its unique elements. Indeed, church growth and development is an art, not a science. What works in Los Angeles may not work in Nashville. What serves a Presbyterian congregation satisfactorily may not help a Baptist body.

I do contend that basic principles can serve the entire body of evangelical churches well, if only we acknowledge them, study them, adapt them, and incorporate them into our planning and operations. Just as the Bible provides certain principles by which we must live, I believe that business can flourish if we recognize and implement the basic, proven principles.

Marketing is a worldly activity. We have been called to be in the world but not of it. Marketing oversteps the boundary.

Marketing *can* overstep the boundary. However, that transgression is the fault of the marketer, not the process. Part of the Christian marketer's task is to remain sensitive to the distinction between marketing that glorifies Christ and builds up His Kingdom and that which is focused on personal or worldly gain. Marketing, just like preaching, is simply an exercise of the gifts and resources that God has provided for our use. I believe God has provided marketing as a systematic approach to use in the ministry of communicating and persuading people.

A Challenge for You

What I offer to you, then, is a perspective on how to make the Church grow and thrive. It is not a foolproof method, nor is it a panacea. Instead, I am providing information about how to perceive your environment and ways to plan, communicate, and develop your ministry. But the success of any method is largely dependent on how the method is employed. So I pray that the information in this book will be the first step toward your understanding of what it means to have a marketing orientation for your church, and that what you learn will motivate you to seriously consider the value of assuming such a perspective for the development of your church.

NOTES: 1. John Sculley, *Odyssey: Pepsi to Apple . . . A Journey of Adventure, Ideas, and the Future* (New York: Harper and Row, Publishers, 1987), page 53.

1
Helping Churches Grow: The Importance of Marketing

The evangelical church in America is losing the battle to effectively bring Jesus Christ into the lives of the unsaved population. I offer this bold statement not for shock value, nor to thrust myself into the role of social prophet of doom. Instead, it is a judgment that comes from my perspective as a professional marketer, and a Christian who is concerned about our ability to reach a needy world.

I base the bold statement on a marketer's most critical tool—information. Consider the following facts, and you will see why I believe the Church is losing its battle to positively and effectively impact this nation for Christ.

Fact: Since 1980, there has been *no growth* in the proportion of the adult population that can be classified as "born again" Christians. (These are people who have made a personal commitment to Jesus Christ, accepting Him as their Lord and

Savior.) The proportion of born again Christians has remained constant (thirty-two percent) despite the fact that churches and parachurch organizations have spent several billion dollars on evangelism. More than 10,000 hours of evangelistic television programing have been broadcast, in excess of 5,000 new Christian books have been published, and more than 1,000 radio stations carry Christian broadcasting. And yet, despite such widespread opportunities for exposure to the gospel, there has been no discernible growth in the size of the Christian Body.[1]

Fact: Since 1970, there has been no appreciable change in the proportion of adults who attend church services at any time during the week. This is true in spite of a growing number of churches, increased church spending for advertising and promotion, and the availability of more sophisticated techniques for informing people of a church's existence.[2]

Fact: The average Protestant congregation in this country has fifty to sixty adults who regularly attend Sunday morning worship services. Generally speaking that is not enough people for a church to prosper—emotionally, financially, or, in many cases, spiritually.[3]

Fact: The fastest growing churches in America are *not* Christian. Among those that are expanding most rapidly are the Church of Jesus Christ of Latter-day Saints (Mormons), Jehovah's Witnesses, and various cults. If you study their operations and the reasons for their growth, you will see that it is because they have effectively used contemporary marketing principles and techniques—without compromising their beliefs and religious practices—in order to build a larger, more participatory membership.[4]

Fact: Attitudinal studies have shown that despite a growing public interest in religion, people's confidence in the church as an institution is declining. Furthermore, only a minority of adults in this nation consider the Christian Church to be "relevant for today." Also be aware that levels of biblical literacy and involvement are on a slow, but steady, decline.[5]

Fact: Community studies conducted in various parts of the country have revealed that a growing number of adults are unfamiliar with the churches in their community. This lack of awareness is not measured by behavioral involvement, such as church attendance, or any kind of intellectual insight, such as doctrinal understanding. The adults I refer to do not even know the names or denominations of the churches in their community, much less what they teach or otherwise offer.[6]

I could continue this list of supporting facts, but the point is clear—the Church is not making inroads into the lives and hearts of people. *My contention, based on careful study of data and the activities of American churches, is that the major problem plaguing the Church is its failure to embrace a marketing orientation in what has become a marketing-driven environment.*

What a Marketing Orientation Means for the Church
What does it mean to be "marketing driven"?

For now, think of marketing as the activities that allow you, as a church, to identify and understand people's needs, to identify your resources and capabilities, and to engage in a course of action that will enable you to use your resources and capabilities to satisfy the needs of the people to whom you wish to minister. Marketing is the process by which you seek to apply your product to the desires of the target population.

If your sensitivity to people's needs causes you to develop ministries that will impact people's lives, you are marketing driven. As a marketing-driven church, you have a consistent desire to know where people are hurting or unfulfilled and to do whatever you can to alleviate their pain and emptiness, for the purpose of building up the Kingdom of Christ.

As a marketing-driven church, you are people centered,

not program centered. You develop a ministry to solve problems, rather than expecting people to force their problems into your mold. You believe that ministry is an interactive, evolving process, not a static structure in which everything can be foreseen and handled via organizational procedures. People have a need to which you respond. Your response changes people, which requires you to devise a new response to their changed condition. Being marketing driven means you are involved in a continuous process—a cycle that does not have a clear starting point and will never have an end point. Why? Because people, whether they are believers or not, will always have needs that the Church can address.

A church with a marketing orientation understands its purpose and its product. (More on this in the next chapter.) Such a church is compelled to get that product to everyone in its environment who needs it. The church may have to adapt its approach in order to reach certain people, but that is part of the marketing process.

What is success in marketing? For a church, it is fulfilling the corporate goals and missions as set forth by the church governing body, in compliance with the mandate of Scripture. Success is helping people grow in their relationship with Jesus Christ.

Churches Are Not Alone in Their Need for Marketing

In conversations with other church leaders, chances are good that you have yet to encounter another leader who talks about his marketing plan or reveals the details of a successful church marketing campaign. You may be inclined to think that marketing is something that only secular corporations do with any aplomb. But this is not so. It is safe to assume that for-profit corporations often have a better understanding of marketing than not-for-profit organizations and that profit-seeking businesses are more likely to perceive marketing as an indispensable business activity than their non-profit counterparts. However, even some of the best-known for-profit organizations have marketing programs that leave much to be desired.

In 1975 Builder's Emporium was a struggling company— a striking example of a company with great potential, but mediocre marketing. They had hundreds of stores throughout the land, but sales were sluggish, the company's image was tarnished, and the probability of future growth seemed remote.

Today, however, Builder's is a thriving, growing, multi-million-dollar giant. What caused the dramatic turnaround? A significant share of the credit must be given to the shedding of their product-driven business philosophy in favor of an aggressive marketing orientation. Under Sanford Sigiloff's able guidance, Builder's has placed the needs of the consumer first, in the belief that satisfying those needs will enable the company to meet its goals and objectives. Instead of placing all their emphasis on the products they felt consumers should want, they started paying attention to what the customers asked for. Once they began providing those products and services, they saw a major reversal of their downward spiral.

Perhaps you have read about the Chrysler Corporation. For several decades, Chrysler was among the innovators in the industry, among the "big three" auto manufacturers. In the 1970s, Chrysler found itself on a roller-coaster ride to oblivion— a rapid decline that brought it to the brink of bankruptcy in 1979. It had been transformed from a successful leader to a crippled also-ran, fighting for its financial life.

Within just six years time, that position of weakness totally reversed. Once again, Chrysler is an innovator, a leader in its field. What made the difference? Shifting its emphasis from manufacturing products that fit its plant capabilities to marketing products and services that satisfied a demand in the marketplace!

Your church can be the Chrysler of tomorrow.

Granted, what we are about to embark upon is an unusual approach to analyzing contemporary ministry. Most books about church growth talk about choirs, parking spaces, forms of preaching, and the role of prayer. Devoting attention to those elements is valuable. However, the approach I take in this book is unusual because we live in an unusual era. Change occurs more rapidly than ever before. Lifestyles are more complicated and splintered than the Pharisees could ever have imagined.

Today, organizational survival requires the ability to evaluate the environment and adapt one's style to keep pace with the changes. Survival does not require compromising one's morals or vision, or the gospel. It does, however, necessitate a clear understanding of the territory within which an individual or organization will attempt to demonstrate those morals and convey that vision.

Four Premises for Marketing the Church Today

Conceptually, this book rests on four key premises.

First, the Church is a business. It is involved in the business of ministry. As such, the local church must be run with the same wisdom and savvy that characterizes any for-profit business. As in the business world, every church must be managed with purpose and efficiency, moving toward its goals and objectives. Our goal as a church, like any secular business, is to turn a profit. For us, however, profit means saving souls and nurturing believers.

Second, I contend that marketing is essential for a business to operate successfully. As I will argue throughout this book, we have to recognize the advantages of marketing and adapt them to the ways of the Church, if we are serious about reaching the world for Christ.

Third, the Christian Church in America, with a few exceptions, does not have a marketing perspective regarding its growth and development. Marketing by default—that is, letting events determine the way in which a product or service is shaped, priced, promoted, and disseminated—inevitably leads to failure by neglect. Sadly, research studies have shown that marketing, as a conscious set of activities growing out of an articulated marketing philosophy, is absent in more than nine out of ten evangelical churches. Most churches, by marketing standards, are failures: that is, they are not maximizing their potential for profit (i.e., ministry gains).

Finally, I believe that many evangelical Christians are sufficiently concerned about the condition of our nation and the state of the Church to seriously consider alternative approaches to building up the Church through the local church body. While the failure to embrace a marketing orientation will not result in the immediate, absolute collapse of the Church, it will prevent the Church from taking advantage of existing opportunities for growth and outreach.

These assumptions form the foundation for the comprehensive strategy for church growth and development outlined in the chapters that follow.

The Marketing Environment We Face

Some people fall asleep by counting sheep. I fall asleep by recounting all the pastors, elders, and other Christian leaders who have, with good intentions, challenged my thesis with the following argument:

> The Church does not need to get involved in marketing. We read the Bible. We pray for God's blessing. We follow the guidance of the Holy Spirit. To rely on modern marketing techniques would be a sign of our acceptance of what the world is doing and our rejection of God's leading. After all, we're engaged in spiritual warfare, not a temporal economic struggle.

This kind of response suggests that we have not yet begun to understand the full parameters of spiritual warfare. It is time we stopped kidding ourselves. Too often, the Church hides behind a spiritual facade that is designed to mask our ignorance, fear, or laziness related to the challenges at hand. This is not to suggest that prayer and trusting the Lord are not key elements to church growth and development; they are absolutely critical, undeniably pivotal. However, we can do more to further the cause of Christ. We, as a Body, have been equipped to do so much more than we have done or attempted to do. I am convinced that God equipped us for a purpose, and that the purpose is to expand the Church. Until we use the resources He has provided, I cannot imagine Him being satisfied with our efforts.

The Church, like it or not, is in a competitive environment. The local church competes with other organizations for the time, attention, money, loyalty—in short, the heart—of people. The real competition is not with other churches—it is with organizations, opportunities, and philosophies that provide people with an alternative to the Christian life. Our main competition is from organizations like ABC, CBS, Universal Studios, MGM, K-Mart, 7-11, JC Penney, and so forth. Those organizations continuously and aggressively seek to permanently place their products, services, and philosophies at the core of the lives of the same people the Church is trying to reach. And organizations like these are highly sophisticated marketers!

For the sake of example, consider Sears. Sears does not care about the spiritual values of its customers—except as they impact Sears' ability to sell merchandise. And that is the point—Sears has a focus on marketing. For Sears, the primary consideration preceding any action in the marketplace is whether or not the action will sell merchandise. Sears does not care whether its activities conflict with the purposes, motives, or desires of a local church, as long as Sears sells its merchandise. Sears is driven by precise goals and objectives. Every set of plans and activities undertaken by Sears is geared toward fulfilling those goals and objectives.

From the Sears' perspective, effective marketing today is the key to being in business tomorrow. Like all major competitors, Sears is playing for keeps. They live by the credo, "May the best marketer win." They take this business seriously: it is not a game. It is the real thing.

How many local churches do you know that are able to compete with the same tough mindedness, the same highly focused sense of purpose, and an equivalent level of professionalism in promoting their ministry (i.e., business) and product as their secular competitors?

If you need further evidence that secular marketers are playing for keeps, take a look at the recent business bestsellers. Their titles convey the seriousness and level of competition: *Marketing Warfare, Guerilla Marketing, Marketing to Win.* This is the mark of an industry that is going for broke. Secular marketers offer no suggestion that they are about to succumb to the Christian Church—which, in their perception, may be a group of kindly, ponderous amateurs who, at best, dabble at the fringes of marketing activity.

A Biblical Context for Marketing the Church

Still, many Christian leaders, when confronted with these facts and perspectives, persist with the notion that marketing is "too worldly," or "not Christian." They view the marketing of a church as a sinful activity, or at least one leading to sin. A credible ministry, they reason, ought not to be tainted by overt marketing.

Enter "Exhibit A" on behalf of marketing for churches: the Bible.

The Bible is one of the world's great marketing texts. No,

it does not clearly list the basic marketing principles. Granted, it does not contain a series of chapters with clearly identified marketing case studies. In fact, the Bible never mentions the word *marketing.*

Perhaps this is what confounds so many Christians about the relationship between marketing and the Church—the absence of the word *marketing* in Scripture. However, the words *abortion, nuclear holocaust,* and *infanticide* are not in the Bible either. Yet we are able to draw conclusions about those activities based on the concepts provided in the Word. Indeed, the foundational concepts of marketing and a myriad of applications are found in the Bible.

The following chapters look at the basics of marketing with greater care. For the purpose of understanding how we can see examples and teachings about marketing in the Scriptures, think of *marketing* as the activities that address the needs of a target audience, thereby allowing the business to satisfy its goals.

I believe that as we begin to understand the basic elements of marketing, we will find countless examples of marketing activity in the Bible. Many of the efforts of Jesus and His disciples represent lessons in marketing and ought to reduce our concern that marketing, as a way of approaching Christian ministry, is not biblically sound.

For instance, an effective marketer must base his plans and tactics on *recent and accurate information.* Rather than relying on emotion and instinct alone, the marketer relies on objective data to provide a realistic picture of the environment and population that he is charged with serving.

If you review Jesus' ministry, you will discover many examples of His mastery of the data gathering and analysis process. Jesus consciously sought to identify people's needs— not by making gross assumptions, but through research (either by questioning the individual, or through keen observation).

He asked the blind man what he wanted. He asked the centurion what he desired. At the Cana wedding, His conversation with Mary uncovered the need for more wine.

The Apostle Paul was another leader in Scripture who understood the value of research in church growth. His entire public ministry was based on a continual environmental assessment. He consistently evaluated the spiritual condition—the need for evangelism, education, and exhortation—of the communities within his jurisdiction. The epistles indicate that the nature and duration of Paul's ministry in a given city was determined by his interpretation of the information he received about the spiritual condition of that place.

Much of this book is devoted to describing the value and process of *marketing planning*. This entails the development of a vision, goals, and objectives, and identifying a viable strategy and set of tactics for reaching those goals. The apostles were early advocates of this approach. Read Acts 6, and notice how they developed a plan for sending out missionaries while leaving other saints behind to attend to the church's material needs.

Jesus Himself taught the importance of planning, criticizing the foolishness of those who failed to plan (Luke 14:28-30). Several of His parables underscore the centrality of strategy and tactics. The parable of the foolish maidens (Matthew 25) teaches us that successful marketing requires anticipating needs and being prepared to satisfy those needs. The parable of the sown seeds (Matthew 13) portrays marketing the faith as a process in which there are hot prospects and not-so-hot prospects and shows how we should gear our efforts toward the greatest productivity. This is the essence of target marketing—recognizing the various segments of the audience, and treating marketing as an ongoing process. Some people are ready for conversion, others are not.

Paul was one of the all time great tacticians. He perpetually studied strategies and tactics to identify those that would enable him to attract the most "prospects" and realize the greatest number of conversions.

Knowing the product and its cost are also integral to the marketing process. Underpricing or overpricing a product can drag a company to its knees in no time flat. Knowing how to determine an appropriate price and how to communicate it are of vital importance.

Jesus Christ understood the price tag of true faith. It was steep, but He was promoting a transaction of great value. Was faith without cost? Absolutely not! Just ask the rich, young man who wanted eternal life, but chose to hold onto his earthly possessions rather than gain heavenly treasures (Matthew 19:16-26). Just ask those seekers to whom Jesus said, "Follow me!" about the extent to which obedience to His command transformed their lives—at the expense of career, family, reputation, and belongings. Indeed, Jesus warned that people following Him would pay a heavy (but fair) price.

Marketing cannot occur without clear and meaningful communication. Modern marketing incorporates various forms of mass communication (radio, television, direct mail) and interpersonal communication. Companies that have not developed means of conveying their message with clarity are rarely successful.

Jesus Christ was a communications specialist. He communicated His message in diverse ways, and with results, that would be a credit to modern advertising and marketing agencies. Notice the Lord's approach: He identified His target audience, determined their need, and delivered His message directly to them. By addressing the crowds on the mountainsides, or the Jews in the Temple, He promoted His product in the most efficient way possible: by communicating with the "hot prospects."

Just as important, Jesus designed the content and language of His message with the nature of His audience in mind. For instance, He spoke very differently to Peter than to Nicodemus, and He conveyed His message to the Pharisees quite differently than to the centurion—even though the message was essentially the same.

Paul provided what I feel is perhaps the single most insightful perspective on marketing communications, the principle we call *contextualization* (1 Corinthians 9:19-23). Paul advocated speaking to people with words and logic that they would understand. He understood that the audience, not the messenger, was sovereign—he was willing to shape his communications according to their needs in order to receive the response he sought.

Another key aspect in marketing is to develop a distribution or delivery system that carries the product to the consumer. If demand for the product exists, but the marketer is incapable of supplying the product, nothing is gained and much, potentially, is lost.

Jesus was well aware of the need to ensure that the faith was accessible to those who sought it. He labored long and hard to turn a motley bunch of working-class men into an informed, capable distribution system. As time passed, His men opened "franchises" (local churches) to further spread the product.

We could spend more time dissecting the Bible to see exactly how the Lord Jesus, the apostles, the prophets, and others in leadership positions utilized basic marketing techniques to further God's Kingdom. However, the point is indisputable: the Bible does not warn against the evils of marketing. In fact, the Scriptures provide clear examples of God's chosen men using those principles. So it behooves us to not waste time bickering about techniques and processes, but to study methods by which we can glorify our King and comply with the Great Commission.

Tangible Advantages of Marketing

Let's make this discussion even more practical. Based on my experience, here are some advantages and benefits a church can realize through effective marketing.

Numerical growth.

If you study your market, devise intelligent plans, and implement those plans faithfully, you should have an increase in the numbers of visitors, new members, and people who accept Christ as their Savior.

Better communications.

Through a planned approach to the message you convey to your target audience (not just through sermons, but through advertising, programs, and other forms of substantive interaction), you can enhance the efficiency and effectiveness of your communications. You should be able to develop the image you want and more persuasively alert people to what you, as a church, are all about, and how they can benefit from what you offer.

Greater understanding of your ministry.

Many churches are diligently ministering, but lack a clear sense of direction or purpose. If you devise your marketing campaign properly, you can overcome this difficulty. By specifying your goals, resources, problems, opportunities, strategies, and tactics, you cannot help but have a very precise definition of why your church is in business and how your ministry can achieve optimum results.

Superior use of resources.

Every church is plagued by limited resources: human, financial, and physical. But these limitations do not have to limit what you can accomplish. If you know exactly where you're going and how you're going to get there, it is much easier not only to conserve your readily available resources and use them more efficiently, but also to identify other needed resources and determine how to acquire them.

Community sensitivity.
A good marketer is in touch with the environment in which he operates. If your church assumes a marketing orientation, you will become better acquainted with the people, problems, and opportunities within the geographic area you serve. Beyond mere awareness of the prevailing conditions, this insight will allow you to make your programs and communications more relevant to people's needs.

More extensive community outreach.
Because of your understanding of the community and the outward perspective a marketing orientation provides, your church will gain wider awareness of the community, have a greater presence for Jesus Christ, provide another option for church seekers, and reap the benefits of a membership that is more involved in personal outreach.

Enhanced personal ministries.
As the people in your church catch the vision and understand the plan for marketing the church, they will have a more meaningful personal ministry if they desire it. The marketing approach enables individuals to take greater ownership of the ministry process, and assume more responsibility, yet it does not overburden them with unwanted or unnecessary spiritual baggage.

New leaders.
What church could not use a new crop of committed leaders to support existing ministries and help shepherd the church into

new areas of ministry? By sharing the vision and developing a planned approach to church growth and development, a new team of leaders can be identified, trained, and involved.

Reduction of the pastor's frustration.
Our surveys have shown that one of the greatest frustrations of pastors is their feeling of being all alone in ministry. By preparing new leaders, by using existing support more effectively, and by developing a plan for managing ministry and growth, the pastor's burden can be better managed, if not largely alleviated. The pastor will never be exempt from ministry pressures, but a well-conceived and implemented marketing effort can ease the tensions involved in making the church reach its potential.

A changed environment.
Once the marketing activity begins to take root, you should notice a different feeling in the church. People should have a better-defined sense of purpose. Generally, the church atmosphere becomes much more positive, upbeat, and confident. The enthusiasm is hard to miss—or ignore.

A Challenge to the Reader
There is no magic formula or routine to follow to yield immediate, wild success in marketing your church. What I hope to convey is simply a new angle on perceiving how—in the midst of a sophisticated, technological, fast-paced, affluent society—you can position your church as a relevant, valuable, and desirable institution for modern man.

The ideas presented in this book are based on marketing data and experience, which is information about people's values and attitudes, insights in the social climate, facts about people's view of the Church and their spiritual beliefs, and studies of marketing strategies and tactics that have and have not worked. With the hope of promoting church growth and development without diluting the Church's fundamental message and goal, I have tried to recast this information to help you reach the people in your community and congregation as cost effectively and meaningfully as might be done by McDonald's, Proctor and Gamble, or American Airlines.

So for the next ten chapters, let's suspend any attachments to traditional thinking about church growth. Let's also enter this journey with a common perspective on the local church. Think of your church not as a religious meeting place, but as a service agency—an entity that exists to satisfy people's needs. We believe that, in the Person of Jesus Christ and the fellowship of the Body of believers, we have the perfect solution to people's needs. We are well prepared to fulfill those needs— not the needs that *we* claim people have, but the needs that people themselves recognize and express. Using the same resources the Church already has—time, talent, money, facilities—how can we squeeze the greatest possible results from those resources and achieve our goals as a service agency in the employ of the God of all creation?

NOTES: 1. Based on research conducted by the Barna Research Group, Glendale, Calif., from November, 1984 to December, 1987.
2. Barna Research Group.
3. Barna Research Group.
4. *Vital Signs,* by George Barna and W. P. McKay (Westchester, Ill.: Good News Publishers/Crossway Books, 1984), pages 119-122.
5. Barna Research Group.
6. Barna Research Group.

2
What Is Marketing?

For several years, my wife was a high school teacher in inner-city schools. She believed that no student should graduate without the ability to write clearly, so she often gave writing assignments to her students. Invariably, the compositions she received fell far short of her expectations. At first she assumed that the students had not given her their best effort. After speaking with her students about their work and discussing the matter with other teachers in the school, she realized that her students had indeed done their best; the problem was, nobody had ever taught them how to write. Her students did not understand the basic principles and techniques of communicating through writing.

I had a similar experience not long ago. I was teaching an introductory course in urban planning at a university in New Jersey. Early in the semester, as a discussion starter, I asked the students to describe the services and design considerations (such as street patterns, building height limitations, and so forth) that they would adopt if they could plan a city from scratch. No takers. Assuming that my question was too convoluted, I rephrased it for them. Still no response.

After an extended, uneasy silence, I asked them why they would not answer a question that was so basic it was almost insulting. It turned out that my students had never thought of a city as a living organism that could be consciously designed and developed. They assumed that cities just evolved, without guidance or forethought. They were dumbfounded by my question because they lacked an understanding of the basic principles of urban development.

My students, and my wife's students, had not failed to perform satisfactorily because they lacked the desire to excel or had an innate inability to master the challenge. They simply had no context in which to understand and analyze the problem. After the problem was identified and the students gained some perspective on the matter, they showed that they were capable of solving the problems.

When it comes to marketing, most local churches are in the same situation as the students I have described. Most churches' inability to grow is not due to a lack of desire, or even a lack of resources. The truth is, we simply have not grasped the basic principles of marketing and applied them to the Church. The opportunities for successful church marketing are plentiful. All we as a community of believers need to do is gain a proper perspective on the Church and how it can be marketed effectively. Then new and exciting doors of ministry will be opened to us.

A Clear Definition
Many people have a bad impression of marketing. Why? Because many people consider *marketing* to be just a fancy

word for *sales*. Even the term *salesman* may conjure up images of middle-aged men with greasy hair in plaid sports jackets trying to sell used cars for double their true value. Many people associate sales and marketing with high-pressure tactics, unscrupulous individuals, and illicit wheeling and dealing.

That is not what marketing is all about. In fact, sales is only one aspect of marketing. Marketing actually involves a broad range of activities such as research, product positioning, awareness development, strategic planning, pricing, advertising, public relations, and audience segmentation. Despite the recent advances in marketing theory and techniques, the basic thrust of marketing is simple: to coordinate related activities intended to make both the producer and consumer satisfied.

Although there is no single definition of marketing that is accepted by everyone, most marketers would feel comfortable with this description:

> Marketing is the performance of business activities that direct the flow of goods and services from the producer to the consumer, to satisfy the needs and desires of the consumer *and* the goals and objectives of the producer.

Notice that marketing is a process—a series of activities—as opposed to a single event. The aim of marketing is to improve the standing of both parties involved. The consumer is helped because his need is satisfied; the producer is helped because his goals are fulfilled. Marketing, then, is merely the activities that enable a transaction to occur that makes both parties better off than they were before the transaction.

The "Four Ps"

To better understand what is involved in making this favorable transaction occur, let's look to the words of some leading marketing educators. One of the pioneers in the marketing education field is E. Jerome McCarthy. In his widely used text, *Basic Marketing,* he describes the "Four Ps" of marketing (product, place, promotion, price).[1] He contends that understanding and intelligently dressing the "Four Ps" is a necessary precursor to successful marketing.

Since my goal is to outline a contemporary perspective on how to market the Church, it is important that you understand the basic foundations of marketing. Without getting into an academic treatment of the discipline, let's briefly examine McCarthy's framework.

The first of the "Four Ps" is your *product.* The product is the entity you offer to consumers to satisfy their need. The word *product* may have connotations that do not do justice to the full range of marketable entities. For instance, a service—life insurance or medical care—is not a tangible item, but is a marketable product. The bottom line, then, is that a product is an entity provided to the consumer to satisfy his needs while enabling you as the producer to meet your goals and objectives.

To successfully market your product, you have to identify its prospective market. The key to market identification—sometimes referred to as "target marketing"—is to be as specific as possible in selecting the audience to whom you will market the product. By matching the appeal of your product to the interests and needs of specific population segments, you can concentrate on getting your product to your best prospects without wasting resources on people who have no need or interest in your product.

To use a simple example, it would be foolish for a hearing aid manufacturer to market its product to the entire adult population, even though that population represents 175 million potential buyers. The manufacturer should know its product well enough to recognize that the majority of the potential buyers will be over age fifty. Thus, by knowing the product's market, the product itself can be developed to address the special needs of that segment, and the entire marketing effort can be designed with maximum efficiency.

The second of McCarthy's "Four Ps" is the *place* related to marketing. This concerns *distribution*, getting the product to the right place for the right audience. In other words, you have to identify where, when, and by whom the product will be transferred to your consumer. Your responsibility is to develop a means of distribution that will provide easy, consistent, and cost-efficient access.

The third "P" is *promotion*. Communicating the nature and availability of the product is essential for marketing success. There are many ways to promote products, and technological breakthroughs steadily create new options. The most common methods of promotion are mass-media advertising (radio, television, newspaper, magazine), direct marketing (mail, telephone), personal recommendations (word-of-mouth), coupons, and trial offers. Without effective promotion, your product does not stand a chance of succeeding, because your target audience will either remain unaware of your product or will not have compelling reason to evaluate or try your product. Promotion is the way in which you persuade people that the product is available, worthy, a good value, and the way you explain how to acquire it.[2]

Last, but certainly not least, is the element of *price*. Determining the price of a product is a complex task, since that decision incorporates an understanding of the actual production, distribution, and promotion costs; the profit margin you need to make the project worth your time and effort; market competition; and the level of consumer demand for your product. Ultimately, the price charged should bring you a fair and reasonable return on your investment and make the product financially accessible and equitably valued for your target market.

Successful products have blended the four aspects of

marketing—product, place, promotion, and price—into an effective mix. If you achieve the proper balance between these elements, you stand a good chance of having a successful marketing experience.

An Orderly Process

One of the beauties of marketing is that it is an orderly process. It is not a series of random, spontaneous actions that magically result in profitable enterprise. Whenever marketing has played a significant role in an episode of business success, that success can be traced to the fact that all of the marketing activities were systematically undertaken in accordance with a preconceived idea of how to approach the opportunities inherent in the environment.

Marketing, then, is a systematic series of active responses to existing conditions that is geared toward reaching specific goals. Although experts differ in their description of the steps in the marketing process, I want to outline a six-step agenda that we will later examine in greater depth.

The initial step is to conduct research that focuses on the consumers' attitudes and behavior. Research might reveal how the consumer might react to a new product, what kinds of consumers have the greatest interest in a particular product, which unmet needs a new product might address, how to most effectively reach and communicate with a specific segment of the audience, and so forth.

The reason for conducting research is to reduce the risk involved in marketing. Research allows you to "get close to the customer." This process, as noted in *In Search of Excellence,* is one of the traits that distinguishes excellent companies from those that are less than excellent. By providing the marketer with objective information about needs and potential responses, research gives solid direction to the marketing process.[3]

Armed with objective data about the marketplace, the

marketer can then develop a *vision,* the second step in marketing. Vision encompasses decisions about what audiences to market to and what kind of product will be developed and offered. Vision is the step that weaves together the factual and creative ends of marketing. Research, the fact-finding process, is creatively analyzed to formulate a perspective on how the company's resources and people's unmet needs can be merged to achieve the company's business goals.

If the product does not already exist, the *production* phase is the third step. The production process provides the marketer with a product that can be brought to the target audience.

But before the product is released, the marketer must have a *marketing plan.* The fourth step outlines not just the marketing team's goals and objectives, but also the strategies and specific tactics by which they will satisfy their goals. The marketing plan is a comprehensive report on the timing, costs, assignment of responsibilities, and methods for assessment related to marketing the product. The marketing plan is the Bible of the marketing game; everything that happens in the life of the product occurs because the plan wills it.

The best plan in the world is worthless, however, unless it is fully *implemented,* which is the fifth step. If the product is to be a success, it must receive the full attention and treatment designated by the plan.

Finally, because marketing is an interactive, flexible process, it has to allow for *feedback* from key sources such as dealers, agents, consumers, and competitors. The underlying concept is that the life of the product can be extended if the marketing is sensitive to market changes and consumer reactions. Once feedback is received, it needs to be processed quickly and accurately, with resulting modifications in the entire process.

These six steps represent the basic marketing activities, which, of course, encompass a variety of strategies and tactics that must happen if the product is to be marketed satisfactorily. The procedures, as a systematic series, are the same whether you are marketing a household product, a church, or a jet airplane. The strategies and tactics would undoubtedly be different, but the basic process is constant.

NOTES: 1. E. Jerome McCarthy and William Perreault, Jr., *Basic Marketing* (Homewood, Ill.: Richard D. Irwin Books, 1987), pages 37-40.
2. Philip Kotler and Alan Andreasen, *Strategic Marketing for Non-Profit Organizations* (Englewood Cliffs, N.J.: Prentice-Hall Publishers, 1987), pages 47-49.
3. Thomas Peters and Robert Waterman, Jr., *In Search of Excellence* (New York: Harper & Row Publishers, 1982), page 14.

3
What Is a Marketing-Oriented Church?

Some ministry leaders consider marketing to be a dirty word, but my perspective is that marketing itself is neither good nor bad; how you use it determines whether it is helpful or detrimental to your ministry. I believe that marketing can be used to great advantage if we keep our eyes on God and trust Him to guide us as we strive to make the Church more effective. I have seen this happen in churches where marketing is considered to be a tool provided by God to further His Kingdom.

Let's now look at how basic marketing principles can be used in God's service and in ministry to other people.

Church Marketing Defined
We can restructure the basic definition of marketing so that it addresses the needs and purposes of the church. In doing so, we might arrive at the following definition:

> Church marketing is the performance of both business and ministry activities that impact the church's target audience with the intention of ministering to and fulfilling their spiritual, social, emotional, or physical needs and thereby satisfy the ministry goals of the church.

The emphasis of this definition is on using marketing to serve the best interests of ministry. While the definition indicates that certain business activities may occur in the process of marketing the church, those activities are undertaken as a necessity to help the church achieve its ministry potential. The practice of marketing has no intrinsic value. For the purposes of the church, its sole value is derived from its ability to enhance church expansion.

As we discuss marketing principles and church applications, you may find that some of your preconceived notions about marketing are a consequence of unfounded assumptions or semantics. If we can get past our unwarranted fears and beyond the terminology trap, I believe you will find marketing to be a logical and sensible approach for your church.

The Common Understanding of Church Marketing

Many clergymen and lay leaders have been exposed to marketing principles. In my travels, I have learned that even the sharpest church leaders who are open to evaluating marketing's potential for church growth, still have a traditional view of the church. They might describe their response to McCarthy's structure in the following way:

> We really don't get involved in marketing, at least not in a pure sense. But we know we need to grow and marketing might be a solution worth studying.
> We don't have to worry about the product, of course, because that's a given. Our product is what

people get on Sunday mornings—a worship service, maybe some Sunday school. Things like the midweek service are an extra, sort of a bonus.

The place is also a given—it happens on the church grounds, in the sanctuary, and in our class-rooms. We've been blessed with this building and we try to use it as efficiently as possible.

Promotion has been one of the elements we strug-gle with. After a lot of discussion in committee, we've decided that advertising in the local newspaper is prob-ably our best approach to letting the community know we exist, announcing the times of our services, and tell-ing people what we're speaking about on a certain Sun-day. We've tried other methods—putting flyers on windshields at shopping centers, bumper stickers, even radio commercials—none of those ever reaped much in the way of results.

The price? No price. God is available to all who seek Him, and He gave His Son as a free gift so that all might live with Him in eternity. We do ask that people support the work of the church with their tithes and offerings, but there is no price tag, *per se,* on attendance.

I suggest that there is a more accurate way to translate McCarthy's principles into a structure that will benefit the church. Let's go back to the beginning, address the basics, and devise a marketing perspective for your church that will enable you to move toward a growth plan.

The "Four Ps" for Church Marketing

The marketing geniuses of today are people like Lee Iacocca, Mark McCormack, David Ogilvy, and Sanford Sigiloff. These men are revered for their clear thinking about the marketing

process and how it relates to their business. Their major successes are a result of knowing and sticking with the most basic
marketing principles.

For those of us who are interested in marketing solely
because of its potential for furthering the church, getting back
to the basics also means looking at Scripture and understanding how examples of marketing characterized the work of Jesus
Christ, the disciples, and the early Church. Don't underestimate the marketing lessons Jesus taught. He understood His
product thoroughly, developed an unparalleled distribution
system, advanced a method of promotion that has penetrated
every continent, and offered His product at a price that is
within the grasp of every consumer (without making the product so accessible that it lost its value).

McCarthy's approach to marketing can help us understand how Christ built the Church, and can lead us to insights
into how we might best be able to further His work today.

Product.
Let's first consider our product. Our product is not the Sunday
morning worship service. That is a *product feature.* (Every
product has *features* and *benefits* that are different from the
product itself.) Sermons, prayers, hymns, and teaching are
some of the features of the church experience. Benefits might
include an increased understanding of the Bible, a sense of
belonging to the community, or the making of new friends
among members of the congregation. These elements are
potentially important in marketing the local church, but they
should not be confused with the product itself.

The real product of the Church is *relationships.* These
relationships occur on two levels. The core relationship is that
developed with Jesus Christ. A relationship with Jesus is the
very essence of Christian ministry. The mission of the Church
is to make believers of all people through a permanent, per-

sonal relationship with Jesus Christ that is both life changing and life giving. The Bible is very clear on this; our purpose is to glorify God through our love for, dependence on, and service to Him. Our relationship with God is made possible through our relationship with Jesus Christ. Nothing is more central to the Christian life or church growth than this relationship.

Our commitment to sharing the love and work of Christ with other people is a significant aspect of our relationship with God. Our relationship with other human beings, then, is our secondary product.

Think back to our definition of marketing. It revolves around satisfying the needs of the consumer. Have you ever met an unchurched individual who craved a sermon? How many people have you come in contact with who were not affiliated with a church, and did not believe in the deity of Jesus Christ, but diligently sought a place where they could sing "The Old Rugged Cross"?

Now think about how many people you know who are looking for meaning in life—something that makes the daily struggles and pressures they face worth the effort. Think about how many people you know, either personally, or indirectly, who are lonely. The national surveys I have conducted over the past several years indicate that loneliness is one of the major, growing problems in America. It is the kind of social problem that the Church needs to identify and respond to. This is what marketing the Church is all about: providing our product (relationships) as a solution to people's felt need.

Is it biblical to look on the product of the Church as being relationships? The experience of the early Church certainly seems to support the notion. Examine the behavior of the early believers outlined in Acts 4. The body of believers grew strong because of their commitment to taking care of each other's needs. They pooled their resources—material as well as spiritual—for the common good.

What about the manner in which Jesus ministered? He was a master at building relationships with people so He could share the gift of salvation with them. Consider His interaction with the Samaritan woman at the well (John 4), or His relationship with the apostles. He never invited people to a church meeting. He never instructed Peter to start a Sunday school class. He built relationships with people and used those relationships as a platform from which to talk about the more meaningful things of life.

Place.

We also have to be more open-minded and creative in our thinking about distribution or place. Many people think of the church as being limited to whatever takes place on the church grounds through the outreach of the professional clergy. This narrow-minded viewpoint is stifling, and it is wrong!

Given a new understanding of our product, thanks to our application of McCarthy's description, we realize that we are marketing an experience that can take place in every corner of the earth. As Christians, whether at work in a grocery store or at a movie theater, we are the Church in action. Regardless of where we are physically, whether the environment is one designed to explore and facilitate relationships with Jesus Christ and other believers or something entirely removed from the spreading of our faith, we are the Church.

The Church is about people reaching and touching other people, so there are no geographic or physical boundaries to that effort. Let's not impose any!

The church building does, indeed, play an important part in local church life. It can be a focal point for an outreach that makes the product real and enables the people in your target audience to grow. But we cannot afford—nor has Christ instructed us—to limit the Church to what takes place between the four walls of your church building.

We also need to explode the myth that ministry is the job of the paid clergy. We are all ambassadors for Christ—ministers in His name—whether we consciously accept that responsibility or not (1 Peter 4:10-11). Expressed differently, every Christian is a marketer working on behalf of the Church. In marketing, it is critical to get the right product to the right target market. For the Church, this means that you and I, and every believer, are the distribution agents. Our task, as outlined in Scripture, is to share our faith with others wherever we are and whenever the opportunity arises.

Promotion.
In thinking about how we *promote* the Church, we have to expand our vision beyond the simple placement of newspaper advertisements or radio commercials. Those elements are useful if properly conceived and placed. Study after study, however, shows that the most believable and best remembered form of advertising is the personal recommendation of a trusted person. Such "word-of-mouth" advertising is ideally suited to the Church. Our product is a relationship involving people. What a smooth fit to promote relationships through the exercise of existing personal relationships!

Research consistently shows that people who have accepted Jesus Christ were led to that conversion experience by the witness of another person. Less than one percent of the "born again" believers in America have accepted Christ as a result of watching evangelistic television. Few have received Christ as their Savior by reading evangelistic magazines and books or listening to evangelical radio programs. Each of those approaches has a place in evangelism and discipleship. However, the key to leading people to accept our core product—salvation through a personal relationship with Jesus Christ—is by establishing and nurturing relationships with other people, with the goal of leading them to explore what the Church has to offer.

Price.
Finally, don't confuse the concept of price with finances. The nature of our product is one in which a financial transaction is superfluous. The type of investment required by the Church is one of commitment—a total personal, emotional, and intellectual commitment to the product. Yes, the local church requires money to operate, but that is not the price of our product. Financial support for the local church is an outgrowth of a person's desire to further spread (i.e., market) the product once the price has been paid.

Talk with unchurched people sometime. You will hear a myriad of reasons why they have not become involved in a local church. Some of those reasons are valid. Some are rationalizations or excuses. But one reason that sometimes arises is the overt thrust of the local church to raise money. (The approach of the television evangelists certainly has not helped our image in this regard!)

Once again, Jesus Christ serves as the premiere example for how to deal with this situation. Jesus walked the streets of Judea and Galilee with little attention given to fundraising. His concern was people's personal commitment to righteousness. Our outreach must have that same thrust, recognizing that righteousness is attained through accepting and following Christ (Romans 3:21, 5:17). The investment all of us need to make is from the heart, not the wallet.

Practical Steps for Marketing the Church
Remember the five steps in the marketing process? Let's see how they apply to marketing a church.

Research.
Research is a critical step for marketing the church. Often we attempt to minister to needs that do not exist while ignoring needs that scream for attention. Unless we take the time and

make the effort to discover—objectively and factually—what people care about, how they hurt, and what service they look to the church to offer, we run a serious risk of being irrelevant and of little value to the people who need what we have to offer.

The absence of research on the needs of the audience is evident in the failure of many existing churches. Sermons address topics that are not pertinent to people's lives. Programs provide training that will not be used. Facilities lie vacant because we are not aware of opportunities for reaching the community. There are a number of ways in which research can be used to clarify how the church can become a more significant servant of the community and how its existing ministry can be improved.

Does this mean your church has to hire market analysts and start conducting weekly telephone surveys? Hardly! You do, however, need a pipeline to the community—a source of continuing, accurate, and fresh information about what is happening and how your church can be a vital part of people's lives. There are simple ways of doing research that are addressed in the next chapter.

Vision.
Vision is a key to marketing the ministry of the church. You may be concerned about my suggestion that vision follows research. Please realize that I am talking about a vision for your marketing effort, not a vision for your ministry. I assume that by virtue of your having read this far, you already have decided that you want your ministry to grow and be alive and exciting. That decision is part of your vision for ministry.

After you have conducted your research and analyzed the facts about people's needs and interests, you can then produce a vision of what your church, through marketing, can become. By understanding the potential available to your church through marketing and tying that into your vision for ministry, you can formulate an entirely new perspective on how your church can reach the community and what kind of influence it can have in the lives of the people you hope to serve.

Unlike a secular organization, in which the product would be manufactured in accordance with the market assessment, the product of the Church has to remain constant. We cannot tinker with our product—how we describe the product, package it, and convey it to our target audience, yes—but the product itself is, so to speak, sacred.

Some churches have attempted to change our product, to make the Church more palatable to the average consumer. This has resulted in a watered-down version of the gospel. Those churches do not really proclaim the saving grace of Christ, and the consumer is not gaining a closer, more meaningful relationship with Jesus Christ. Instead of marketing becoming a win-win situation in which both parties emerge better off than before the marketing activity took place, compromising the product has resulted in a lose-lose condition where both the church and its followers are in a worse place than before, since they have been deceived into believing that they have found the keys to life and spiritual meaning.

Our product is the development of a relationship with Jesus Christ and the development of secondary relationships with believers, regardless of what the marketing process looks like. Thus, while the Church does not have to worry about conceiving, shaping, producing, and revising a new product, we would do well to remind ourselves exactly what our product is and take every precaution to be certain that we are not in any way, shape, or form changing the product to suit our environment.

Marketing plan.
The marketing plan becomes a key instrument for marketing the church. As we set out to compose a plan, we have to assess

the resources available to us, and the nature of our goals and objectives, then devise a reasonable yet challenging course of action. Our plan should include the strategies and tactics necessary to reach our goals and objectives, along with an accounting of how much time, money, and labor will be required to achieve the plan.

The marketing plan may be no different, in concept and detail, from a well-formulated ministry or missions plan. It should be specific, comprehensive, and stand as a document that the church leaders will refer to as the benchmark against which all marketing efforts are measured.

Implementation.
A church is no better off having a marketing plan than not having one unless enough enthusiasm and manpower can be mustered to put the plan into action. Unlike secular marketing organizations, a church may have to rely almost exclusively on volunteer assistance. This might mean that the pace at which the church is marketed is more deliberate than would be the case if resources were not a consideration. However, the thoroughness of the implementation and the quality with which the marketing activities are done are more important than the speed of the marketing process. If we are going to market our church, let's do it right, or let's not do it at all. We will make mistakes, but let them be unintentional execution errors rather than miscues resulting from irresponsibility or a lack of caring.

Feedback.
Feedback is so important for us to incorporate into the process! If we are nothing else, we should be sensitive to the feelings and perceptions of those who are working for the benefit of the church as well as those to whom the church wishes to minister. Naturally, feedback is only worthwhile if we have a system for

translating that information into a structured response. The input we obtain from those impacted by our marketing efforts should serve to make us better marketers and ministers. In short, the church should continually be more effective at marketing with each passing day, as we learn from our mistakes and build on our successes.

We Are Different

I grant you that the Church is at a disadvantage compared to the marketing position of most secular organizations. Church leaders usually enter the church marketing process with little or no training in marketing, armed with virtually no budget for marketing, and have to rely on volunteers to enact the marketing plans. But do not despair. At least four elements distinguish church marketing from consumer product marketing, and those four differences are cause for celebration.

First, we have the benefit of the Bible, which is a source of guidance. As we prepare our plans and tactics, we can refer to Scripture for inspiration and direction. We can study the work of Jesus and His disciples to understand how they approached a doubting society. The pages of Scripture remain a yardstick against which we can measure the validity and integrity of our plans.

Second, we have the power of prayer behind us. No church should enter the marketing process without turning to God in prayer, seeking His power and guidance. And no church should accept any marketing plan, regardless of how sophisticated or comprehensive it might be, without offering it to God for His blessing. Through our prayers we can overcome obstacles that would confound more experienced and schooled marketers. Through our prayers we can involve God as a partner in church marketing.

Another advantage is that the people within the church who are asked to assume marketing responsibilities are not in competition with each other. In fact, the church must view the marketing process as an opportunity to open up ministry to all who seek to support the church. Marketing provides a chance to include all people who have gifts that can be incorporated into the process. Since we do not treat the marketing of the church as an opportunity for personal gain, church marketing affords every person who becomes involved an opportunity to further the church through the unique gifts and talents that the Lord has bestowed on each of us.

Finally, we are freed from the bondage of using money as our scale of success. While corporations engage in marketing for the purpose of accumulating tangible wealth, we seek a higher end—the spiritual advancement of God's people. With that goal in mind we will not become enslaved to the marketing process out of lust for earthly treasure, and we should not lose our enthusiasm for the activities because we have no stake in the outcome. Our motivation ought to spring from the fact that our efforts will result in more effective ministry and superior service to God. If we refrain from getting caught up in the numbers game and keep our focus on the purpose of ministry, we will find church marketing to be a satisfying challenge.

4
Understanding the Market:
The Importance of Information

U p to this point we have spoken about the marketing process in broad, conceptual terms. Given the steps that have
been outlined in the marketing process, let's now explore how
to translate those general concepts into specific efforts that
will lead your church to the cutting edge of growth.

In marketing, the systematic gathering and analysis of
information is usually referred to as research. Perhaps the
best-known market researcher was the late George Gallup, Sr.
The Gallup poll has become an ingrained institution in America, widely recognized as a reliable barometer of people's feelings, beliefs, and behavior.

Despite all of the sophistication built into the Gallup poll,
I would argue that you are, in many ways, just as experienced a
marketing researcher as was George Gallup.

Another outrageous claim? Not really. If you understand

that marketing research is merely the collection and analysis of information in order to make better decisions, the process seems less elusive. Consider, for instance, two common activities that qualify as simple exercises in marketing research:

> When you read newspaper advertisements for several supermarkets, comparing the brands and prices of each before deciding what products to buy at which stores, you have conducted a small-scale survey, most likely leading to a better decision.
>
> When you seek to purchase an automobile, chances are good that you will visit several dealers before you make a purchase. In so doing you have researched your target market (perhaps defined by automobile make and the geographic proximity of the dealers you were willing to visit) and made the optimal selection, based on the body of information you were able to collect and evaluate.

It has been said that we are living in the Age of Information. That may well be. As the United States has evolved from a manufacturing-based nation into a service-based economy, information has become the basis of the economy. Conditions have changed so dramatically that the course on quantitative research methods at one major university has been revised so that only a single equation must be memorized by students. Replacing literally dozens of mathematical equations that are now done by computer, a single equation summarizes the present-day situation: information equals power.

The truth embodied by that formula is in wide evidence: Those who possess and utilize information most effectively are those who stand the greatest chance of succeeding in the marketplace.

The value of information for Christian churches is no less

significant than for major profit-seeking corporations. Every day church leaders are responsible for making important marketing decisions that will determine the future of the local church body. It is every bit as critical for church leaders to base their decisions on an informed understanding of the marketplace as it is for the marketing executives at corporate giants like Campbell's Soup or Ford Motor Company to do so. (It is even more important when you consider the spiritual significance of the Church's outreach compared to the temporal significance of the typical consumer product.) Rest assured, those marketing executives would not dare launch a new product or advertising campaign, recommend a new site for manufacturing, suggest a product price change, or aim future marketing efforts at a new population segment without a serious study of the available information related to such a decision.

Common Objections to Research Overruled
You are not the first church leader to whom I have presented this argument. Frequently, however, I have found that church leaders "turn off" at this point. Some are still troubled by the concept of using business techniques to enhance the local church. I assume that if you have gotten this far, that is not a potential problem. Other common objections to information gathering and use include the following:

A local church does not have the budget to sustain any kind of meaningful marketing research effort. Thus, there is no sense in taking this discussion any further. Learning rudimentary research methods and strategies without having the financial means to implement them would be like teaching French to a person with a noncommutable life sentence: stimulating, perhaps, but ultimately impractical.

Pastors go to seminary, not MBA programs. They have no training in marketing research. Other church personnel are just as unprepared for hands-on research activity. Hence, even if the church saw the value of marketing research as an integral part of marketing itself, nobody on staff could carry that load. It would be embarrassing to watch the average market researcher give an exegetical sermon. It would be every bit as sad to review the marketing research conducted by the average pastor.

These are valid concerns. Because churches are not run like businesses, very few congregations actually budget for research. Similarly, given that seminary training does not generally include courses in marketing or marketing research, it is rare for a pastor to enter the ministry with any formal background in research techniques.

However, the approach I am about to outline for you takes these limitations into account. Don't forget, this is the Age of Information. Seven out of every ten employees in this country work in service-oriented jobs, many of which entail the collection and analysis of information. The Age of Information means we live in an era in which an abundance of information—facts, figures, forecasts—already exists. Using the resources already available, it is possible to develop a viable church research effort. Naturally, if your church allocates funds for research, more extensive and sophisticated work can be conducted. However, neither failure to budget for research, nor lack of training among the pastoral staff need relegate a church to the status of "information ignoramus."

How Can the Church Use Information?

Have you ever been involved in a church meeting in which a major decision was going to be made, but was made difficult by a lack of adequate information? Examples of such situations might clarify the point.

A church is considering the wisdom of erecting a new school building. It has determined that the money can be raised, but the question is whether it should be done. Absent from the discussion are pieces of information such as a forecast of the number of children who will be living in the community in the next decade, statistics regarding the likely use of such facilities, the attitudes of people toward expensive church building projects, and the impact of a larger campus on the image and expectations of the church.

The elders have decided that it is time for an aggressive campaign to add new members to the congregation. The discussion, however, centers on people sharing their personal opinions on the wisest course of action. Nobody has taken the time to profile the local population—their demographics, lifestyles, and attitudes—to better understand what might naturally attract people. There is no reliable base of information to explain why current church members are attending the church—thus giving some indication of the church's strengths that might be capitalized on in an outreach campaign. No systematic examination of what is and is not working in nearby churches—a case study approach—has been done to provide ideas for consideration.

The local church, like every other organization responsible for marketing a service or product, is constantly making decisions that place the organization at risk: decisions about how the product is made, decisions about how it will be distributed, decisions about the price of the product and how it will be promoted, decisions about new product ideas and the organization's image. Every time a new decision is made, the success of the organization is potentially jeopardized, depending on how intelligently the decision is made.

The purpose of marketing research is to provide information that, when properly collected, analyzed, and interpreted, will minimize the decision-making risk to the organization. Two of the most common uses of marketing research are for exploring new opportunities and gaining feedback on how adequately the organization is doing its job.

Generate and test new ideas.
Information is the catalyst for creating concepts for products or services. By examining information about people's behavior, attitudes, needs, and desires, marketers often come up with brainstorms about how to better serve the public while making a profit for the company—the essence of good marketing. Once a creative thought has been inspired, that idea can then be further researched to ensure that it has sufficient potential to warrant the resources required to develop and market it.

Evaluate performance.
Marketing research is frequently conducted to assess how adequately a company is satisfying the needs of its target audience. This might entail an examination of people's reactions to the company's products, either in relation to the products of competitors or in comparison to how well the company performed on a similar evaluation in the past. Performance evaluation could also involve measuring the effectiveness of advertising or the nature of a company's image.

The results of such research can be valuable in helping organizations set realistic goals and determine how they can most effectively go about meeting their goals.

Collecting Existing Information for Church Research
As mentioned earlier, the local church is in a competitive environment. It may not have a six-figure budget for marketing research, nor a staff of highly trained, experienced, research analysts. That, however, is no excuse for failing to recognize the need to integrate reliable information into its marketing activities and actively pursue that integration.

A powerful information tool available to every church is what is called *secondary data*. This is information that has already been collected by another person or organization (probably with a different use in mind) that can provide useful insight. Best of all, secondary data is usually available to interested parties for minimal, if any, cost and can be obtained relatively quickly. Some examples of secondary data include:

- Demographic reports developed by the Bureau of the Census and available through your city government;
- Attitudes and lifestyle information for community residents, collected as part of a survey of readers of your metropolitan newspaper;
- Magazine and newspaper articles describing the results of public opinion polls about current issues and felt needs;
- A population forecast prepared by the research department of a university or denomination.

As our society continues to place a premium on information, secondary data is more readily available. The disadvantage of secondary data is that you have no say in how the study is conducted or what kinds of information are collected. The advantages, however, are the minimal cost and immediate availability.

As a marketing-driven organization, the local church ought to have several people who are responsible for thinking about and sifting through the wealth of secondary information flooding the marketplace to identify and store that which is of value to the marketing of the church. For this effort to have maximum value, four key steps should be followed.

Assign the responsibility.
Unless this task is specifically outlined and assigned to one or more individuals, it will not be done properly. Ideally, the collection of secondary data should be done regularly according to a planned approach. However, rest assured that it will not be done at all unless a person or group within the congre-

gation accepts ownership of the project.

The number of volunteers incorporated into this project depends on their commitment and resources. In some cases, one person may wish to do it all and will prove to be capable of handling the responsibility. In other cases, a dozen people may be involved, each one responsible for monitoring information in a single publication that they normally read anyway.

This task represents a wonderful opportunity for people to ease into the concept of church marketing. Anyone who reads a newspaper or magazine could potentially become part of the information-gathering system. People might be asked to cut out articles on specific topics or collect certain pieces of information for a six-month period. Other individuals might be asked to collect articles and information from the readers, and integrate that data into the church information system. If done with imagination and care, this process could truly develop a more committed cadre of church members—a group that is subtly introduced to church marketing and provides a valuable service to the church leadership.

Specify the information interests of the church.
There is more information flowing through the marketplace than anyone could reasonably hope to keep up with. To make sense of it all, and to avoid burning out church leaders who volunteer their time and energy to help, it is necessary to provide a very clear-cut list of information that should be tracked. For instance, a church might wish to keep track of survey data related to people's felt needs, reactions to political and social issues, and changes in lifestyles; new demographic patterns concerning the population's age distribution, changes in the family structure (e.g., single parents, working women, unwed mothers), levels of household income, and rates of population growth by racial groups; and information about church attendance and membership.

By providing a well-defined body of information that will be valuable to the church leaders in making decisions, it is easier for the information gatherers to find and record such facts and figures. It is also critical that a simple system be developed to pass on new information to the church leaders who would use the information in their decision-making processes. This not only makes the information worth collecting, but provides a sense of accomplishment and purpose for the people collecting it. Once again, though, unless a structure for sharing that information is developed, the chances are that much of the collected information will never see the light of day, resulting in an exercise in futility.

Develop a system for cataloging the information.
While the body of information that is uncovered for the church may not rival the Library of Congress for depth or volume, it must be managed in such a way as to allow access for those who need the information. Inaccessibility is tantamount to not having the information. The cataloging of information should be simple so that anyone new to the system can figure out how to find information without difficulty.

There are a myriad of ways in which information can be logged. You may have an individual file folder for each issue or type of information collected. You may have a notebook in which pertinent facts are logged. You may develop a file card system on which information is stored. The possibilities are endless. The important factor is accessibility, ease-of-use, and consistency in information storage.

Limit the data search to the most fruitful sources.
There are more than 10,000 magazines published in this country. Nearly every neighborhood is served by a community newspaper, one or more metropolitan newspapers, and the three national, daily newspapers. Several thousand research

reports are released by companies each year, with countless more available from local, state, and federal governments. It is impossible for a church to keep up with such a mountain of information. Even attempting to do so will lead to frustration and wasted resources.

Perhaps the wisest approach is to pinpoint for your research team (i.e., the handful of people responsible for regularly collecting available secondary information) not only the topics of greatest interest to the church, but the sources of information that are most likely to provide the kinds of facts desired. For instance, you may decide that the research team should limit its search to a regular perusal of journals such as *Public Opinion, American Demographics, Newsweek, USA Today, Marketing Week, Advertising Age,* and *Christianity Today* (all of which, by the way, are available at most public or college libraries).

It is important to keep a reasonable perspective on this project. You will not wind up with the world's most comprehensive and sophisticated data base. Your goal is simply to keep abreast of information that will enable the church to minister more effectively.

Constantly review the information objectives set forth. If you want information on people's needs so that sermons can touch more relevant topics, do not allow the research team to become sidetracked and collect peripheral data. If one of the information objectives is to understand population trends, make sure that the objective is specific enough to preclude people wasting precious time tracking down insights on population trends that are of no value to your church (e.g., the number of television sets owned by people in rural versus urban areas).

Do not let the research team bear the burden alone. Part of the church marketing orientation ought to include an understanding among all lay leaders that when they become aware of a new trend or interesting piece of information, which may impact the way in which the church ministers, they should pass that information along to the research team or appropriate committee.

Indeed, one of the greatest assets of any church is the diversity of its members. That diversity is evident in many ways—including the range of publications and sources of information to which those members are exposed. By simply asking church leaders to keep an eye open for information that might keep the church on the cutting edge of what is happening in the marketplace, not only will useful information be brought forth, but there will be a wider sense of ownership. The church will benefit from the more widespread feeling of involvement in the marketing of the ministry.

Collecting Primary Data for Church Use
The most current and church-specific information, however, would come from *primary data*. This is information derived originally by, and for, the church itself. For instance, when a magazine conducts a reader survey, that is an example of primary research—new information gathered by the publication that is designed to help market the magazine more effectively. Examples of primary research are increasingly common. In political campaigns, candidates often commission periodic public-opinion polls to keep track of how they are doing in the race and which hot issues they ought to be discussing (or avoiding!). Before IBM launches a new line of computers, it conducts a series of primary research studies to identify consumer needs and to obtain reactions to product ideas and prototypes. In the same way, the church needs to be "beating the bushes" to find out how its target audience responds to its ideas and activities.

Realizing that few churches budget any money for research (an oversight that needs to be corrected), we will focus on three pieces of research that can be done inexpensively, but have a potentially explosive impact on the life of the church.

Seek out the opinion elite.
One method of gaining insight into what is happening locally that the church needs to be aware of is to seek the input of the local "elite." In every community a small cadre of opinion leaders and opinion recorders exists. By having key marketing people from your church talk with these people on a regular basis, the church will address two vital marketing needs: the need for information and the need to communicate an image of sincere concern to key community leaders.

Who are the opinion elite? In most communities, having an open and running dialogue with the following officials would be invaluable:

- *Local political officials*—the mayor, city council members, state assemblymen, Congressmen;
- *Journalists*—editor of the community newspaper, news anchor for the local radio station;
- *Educators*—high school principal, school superintendent;
- *Law enforcement officials*—chief of police, local magistrate;
- *Business leaders*—president of the Chamber of Commerce, leaders of civic groups like the Jaycees, Lions, or Rotary.

The underlying purpose of contacting these leaders is to gain an informed outsiders' perspective on what is happening in your area. Beware, however, not to take any one person's perspective as the absolute truth. What you are gathering is "qualitative" information—that is, the viewpoint of one individual that does not, by itself, constitute a representative, statistically defensible picture of the environment. Use the insights gained to give you ideas, to sharpen your sensitivities to what is taking place, to give you yet another piece of data that can be used to develop a holistic perspective on the heart and soul of the community you are striving to reach.

As you can imagine, gaining the perspective of the elite can be a time-consuming or expensive process. It should not become such a burden. You might want to regularly touch base with each person in your elite core once every six months or so. You might do so in a friendly, non-threatening atmosphere, such as over breakfast at a local restaurant. At the same time, remember that you are promoting your product—conveying an image of your church, building a relationship with the individual, and perhaps moving closer to the appropriate time to invite that person to explore your faith.

The more complex strategies for gaining information involve *quantitative* data. This refers to information that is statistical in nature, where the story is relayed through numbers. Don't let the prospect of collecting a myriad of statistics scare you. Although such research must be done carefully and with a certain level of methodological sophistication, it can be done without losing simplicity or the desired level of insight into the strengths and weaknesses of your church. Realize too, that much like the secondary research effort, this task should not be done by a single person in the church. It works best when it is a team effort.

Conduct a congregational survey.
One of the two quantitative approaches I recommend is a *congregational survey.* The objective is to gain feedback on how well the church is meeting the needs of the people who attend it. These people are the base from which the church must grow. If the church is not being satisfied internally, there is little hope of reaching out to incorporate others into the

body. A congregational survey can help identify how well the church is doing and highlight those areas of need that are not being satisfactorily addressed.

Dozens of textbooks have been written on how to conduct surveys. Unless your church has someone in the congregation with expertise in this area, you might wish to consider seeking the assistance of professionals. These professionals are located in the following places:

- A nearby Christian college where professors who teach business, sociology, psychology, or political science may be able to help;
- A Christian consulting firm, which may have special arrangements for local churches (see list in chapter eleven);
- Denominational offices, which may have a specialist to help design and conduct the survey, or may be able to provide a list of capable experts available to your church.

The desired end result is to have all members and visitors who attend the church complete a questionnaire at a single point in time (e.g., on a predetermined Sunday morning). They would fill out a questionnaire describing their experiences and involvement with the church; their satisfaction with various services, programs and facilities; and their expectations and hopes for the future.

The survey is a feedback tool, a resource for identifying what the church has done well, what it has done poorly, and what opportunities it has yet to take advantage of. Only through the examination of objective, reliable input can the church realistically evaluate how it is doing. And only through consistent, honest self-evaluation can the church hope to become more effective in ministry.

Conduct a community survey.
Another source of important primary data is the *community survey*. This is conducted with a random sample of community residents to determine how adequately the church is being marketed to the community. Are people aware of the church? Do they understand what it stands for? What is the general impression of the congregation? Does the church seem relevant and contemporary? If a person was interested in attending a church, what are the chances that he would consider that particular church? What kind of issues and personal needs should the church be addressing through its sermons and programs? These types of questions can provide useful guidance in assessing the work of the church and how its efforts need to be reshaped or promoted.

Once again, the methodology and mechanics are best left to individuals who have the experience to justify the resources. The key is to obtain the information on a regular basis (perhaps every two years) to fine tune the outreach and ensure that it is meeting needs.

Using the Information to Market the Church
A key mistake many marketing organizations make is to have the right systems but fail to use them properly. In other words, it will do no good if information about the marketplace is collected, cataloged, and even analyzed, but is not incorporated into the thinking and decision making of church leaders. It is critical that information be used to enhance the manner in which the church is growing. Information is not an end in itself: it is a means to an end, which is the improvement of the church's ministry.

Someone in the church has to initially accept the role of championing the research process. That person should have a clear sense of the value of information, the ability to manage people and information, and a realistic philosophy of how a local church can use information to better serve people. The individual need not be a research expert. He or she must, however, understand how information can be utilized to create a more aware, sensitive, and effective church. The degree to which a church research program is effective is due to that individual's ability to provide leadership to other church members involved in collecting, cataloging, and analyzing information.

Let's consider a simple example. The pastor is concerned that the people do not consider his sermons to be relevant. The feedback he has received from people is that he is preaching about topics that are too theological and not practical enough. His concern is twofold. First, he is not spiritually feeding his people. Second, he knows that if his own congregation is not satisfied with what they are getting, they will not invite friends and associates to visit the church, thus stunting the church's growth potential. Indeed, if members become frustrated enough, they may leave the congregation and further disrupt the church's potential ministry.

The research team is therefore instructed to identify issues that are "hot" locally—things that would be on people's minds and on which a sermon would be both timely and personally helpful.

Assuming that the team does not have the ability to conduct either a congregational or community survey, it would turn to secondary research. It would scour local newspapers to determine which issues and topics are receiving the greatest attention. It might go to the library and look up the most recent Gallup and Harris polls to find out the kinds of issues addressed and the prevailing public sentiment. It might evaluate the topics on which articles in recent regional and local magazines were published. The end result for the pastor might be a list of half a dozen or more issues of current prominence, providing a basis for a series of sermons.

It is possible that the church might wish to use the information even more broadly, determining how the church might translate the information into outreach. For instance, if alcoholism emerged as a primary issue of interest and concern, the church might consider the following strategy:

- Promote a series of sermons on alcoholism;
- Initiate a student education program, perhaps conducted through the public school system;
- Sponsor a series of weekly seminars, open to the general public, featuring outside speakers addressing the topic;
- Contact the local police department to both offer the support of the church and to ask if there are ways in which the church could work with the police in combatting alcoholism;
- Place posters that deal with the dangers and solutions to alcoholism on church walls.

When such action is taken, however, remember that the actions resulting from research are meant to be conducted in conjunction with the church's overall marketing strategy and tactics. Never lose sight of the fact that every move the church makes impacts its marketing efforts. All actions should be coordinated with the marketing vision as much as possible.

Research Is Not a Panacea
Some people make the mistake of thinking that marketing research can solve all of an organization's problems. That is an unrealistic expectation. The role of research is to provide an objective series of facts that require a subjective interpretation. Research is meant to be one of several inputs into the decision-making process. For the Christian, the guidance of the Holy Spirit must also be integrated into the decision-making proc-

ess. Experience in ministry and marketing needs to be woven into the decisions being made. My observation has been that churches using a balanced combination of information, experience, and prayerful consideration of God's leading are the ones that minister and grow most efficiently.

It is important to recognize the place of research in marketing the church. A church that does not collect and analyze valid data cannot truly know whether or not it is meeting people's needs. And a church that does not meet needs is not in the business of ministry.

5
Creative Thinking About Marketing and Ministry: The Importance of Vision

Without vision, you cannot be successful in marketing. This is true whether you are marketing cereal, automobiles, computers, or a church. If you are serious about marketing your church successfully, you must start with a clear vision.

Sadly, it is uncommon for a church to be led by a man or group of people who have a well-focused vision. Experience has shown that, more often than not, churches that consistently grow and have the greatest ministry impact are those that have operated in accordance with a vision for their ministry.

The Lack of Vision

In my work with churches around the nation, I have seen two underlying reasons why churches seem paralyzed when it comes time to respond to problems and opportunities.

In some churches, rigor mortis has set in because the pastor is not willing to relinquish control long enough to allow others to have a stake in the church's ministry. Although there may be able and willing people to assist the pastor in his quest for church growth and development, he is either too insecure to permit such assistance or is not able to manage people effectively (to properly utilize their gifts and talents).

Other churches suffer from the lay people's failure to become excited about ministry and take an active part in the church life. For many years they have been involved in churches where their mere presence on Sunday morning was considered virtuous and only the spiritual giants were expected to or were capable of performing the "deeper" tasks such as teaching Sunday school or leading a Bible study.

In all these churches, the problem is not a lack of ability, for God provides all the talent needed to enable His Church to prosper. The missing link is not money, for the Church in America today raises and spends more money than McDonald's and Sears Roebuck combined. The problem is a lack of vision.

What Is Vision?

My research indicates that most Christians have no sensitivity to the importance of vision in ministry, or in their own lives Also, few churches consciously strive to impart a sense of vision for ministry to the people. Indeed, when the term *vision* is employed, people often think of individuals who live on the charismatic end of the Christian continuum—those people who see mystical images and proclaim grandiose revelations from God as a consequence of their personal experience of God's extraordinary contact.

This, however, is not the kind of vision I am extolling. When I refer to vision, I'm talking about a comprehensive sense of where you are, where you're going, and how you're going to get there. I'm talking about seeing "the big picture," a portrait of all that exists in your sphere of potential influence, and developing a concept of how you and your organization fit within the aggregate environment.

Yet vision is more than developing a mental picture of the past, present, and future. Vision is also the driving force behind the activity of a motivated leader or group of people. Vision is the internal force that guides an individual through unforeseen difficulties or stimulates a person to act when he is too tired or ambivalent to take the next step toward reaching the goal. Vision is the characteristic that is the responsibility of a leader and sets the leader apart from his followers. The leader has and communicates the vision; the followers accept and help carry out the vision.

Note that vision is not naturally possessed by everyone. Vision is a gift bestowed on some people who generally rise to positions of leadership and authority. Also, vision must be communicated. The key to making vision useful is for its possessor to share it with those who do not possess it, but who can support it.

Expressed differently, I am talking about the kind of vision that differentiated the Apostle Paul from other biblical characters. Paul visited the churches of Galatia, Philippi, Ephesus, and elsewhere because he had a clear-cut perspective of what the Church must become in order to be pleasing and useful to God. Paul was passionate about his vision and was not able to rest until he saw it fully realized. God provided Paul with a vision of the Church, and Paul was relentless in his pursuit of that vision.

I believe the Bible also shows us people who had no vision and thus were left behind without making a positive mark on the world. The Pharisees and Sadducees, for the most part, lacked vision. Their perspective was so narrow, antiquated, and inflexible that they could not progress. Pontius Pilate was a man who lacked definite vision. He was a functionary—doing the routine work required of his position, but who seemed to lack a comprehensive perspective on the world of which he was a part.

Contemporary Men of Vision

In marketing, it is interesting to note that a person of vision leads nearly every company that is either successful or on the cutting edge of progress. The leaders of these companies feel challenged by the world around them and feel compelled to make their mark on the world through the force of their own ideas, personalities, resources, and desires.

Let's look at a few examples of men with vision.

William Norris is the founder of Control Data, one of the world's giants in the computer industry. Norris has a vision of solving societal needs by conducting his business in ways that will provide solutions to common urban problems. Toward that vision he has moved six of Control Data's plants to inner cities, created numerous small business centers, provided educational opportunities (via computer) to prison inmates, and trained and hired several thousand uneducated and otherwise disadvantaged people who lived in dilapidated urban centers. Control Data has remained highly profitable while making a substantial impact on the lives of thousands of people who previously had little hope for meaningful lives. Over the years, Norris has been the object of scorn and ridicule, but he has persevered against the odds and come out a winner. Why? He had a vision, and he stuck with it.

Steve Jobs, the founder of Apple Computers, moved into IBM's forsaken turf. Working with cohort Stephen Wozniak, Jobs set forth to make computer technology user-friendly—a new concept in computer application. He believed that if the technology could be harnessed and made both intellectually and emotionally accessible to the average person, the market would expand like hot cakes. Industry experts felt the idea was interesting, and that if it were possible, IBM would be the one to do it.

At the time he launched his challenge to IBM, Jobs was an unknown upstart in his twenties, a person without any viable corporate training or experience. He took on IBM, the industry leader, although few people figured he was anything more than a dreamer. After years of testing and developing, Apple became a major player in the computer market, a multibillion-dollar corporation currently challenging IBM's supremacy. Jobs had managed to translate his dream into reality. How? By following his vision for what the future could offer.

The air freight industry offers another compelling example. For many years, packages that needed to be delivered as rapidly as possible were sent via passenger aircraft. Elaborate preparations had to be made and the process was cumbersome, expensive, and not terribly reliable. Worse, it took two, three, and sometimes even four days for those all-important packages to reach their destination. Fred Smith believed there was a market to be served and that a more efficient way to handling air freight was achievable, so he conceived a way of providing overnight package delivery. Defying his critics, Smith built Federal Express into a billion-dollar business, the leader in a fiercely competitive industry. Talk with Smith and you find a man who was able to keep going, and to motivate his staff to hang on during the dark times, because he had an unshakable vision of what his service could become.

Vision is not limited to business operations. I have met and followed the activities of various Christians who had a vision and implemented it. They are, by any standard, winners.

Bill Hybels was a youth pastor in Illinois. He had a vision for reaching the unchurched adults in his area. He conducted research, planned a creative marketing strategy for starting a new church geared to the needs of his community, and launched Willow Creek Community Church. Less than a decade after its first worship service, Hybels' congregation now numbers some 10,000 people every Sunday. Most members of his congregation are people who were not attending church—and had no incentive to do so—until Hybel's vision became a reality.

Pat Robertson began CBN with only a few dollars in his pocket and a vision. Today, his vision has expanded to include the CBN Cable Network, one of the largest and more successful cable networks in the country; CBN University, a school dedicated to training Christians in journalism; and a variety of other ministries that reach millions of people around the globe. At the outset, few people believed Robertson had a chance at doing anything special, given his limited resources. He was sustained by his vision of how God could use him and various forms of technology to reach millions of people with the gospel.

I have also known and worked with people who are less well-known but who have a powerful vision of how God desires to use them, and have been faithful to that vision. Stefan Bankov labored for nearly a decade to develop a concordance written in the Slavic language for pastors behind the Iron Curtain. Despite a lack of sufficient funds and staff, Bankov completed that volume and has been able to distribute thousands of copies in several Slavic nations.

Dick Innes was a builder by trade, in Australia, when he felt God leading him to develop a nationwide literature ministry. In a short span of time, he mobilized the resources to reach every home in the outback and rural sections of Australia with high-quality, gospel literature. Thousands of people who had never visited a church or read the Bible came to accept Jesus Christ as their Savior. Innes has since come to the United States with the vision of reaching this nation, Canada, and England with meaningful, needs-oriented, gospel literature. I would never bet against Innes, because he is a man of vision.

I am captivated by the realization that success in ministry is a result of vision, not a prerequisite for vision. Another inescapable, factual conclusion is that successful churches, like profitable business enterprises, must be led by people of vision.

How Can Vision Be Developed?

A number of similarities characterize the lives of men who have made it to the top of their profession or have had a significant impact on the world. It seems that a person of vision is:

Creative.
Often, vision is not accompanied by unlimited resources to fulfill the vision, which requires some novel approaches to the obstacles that might prevent the execution of plans to accomplish the vision. Fulfillment of vision requires the ability to shake off the fetters of convention and devise unusual or unique ways to get things done.

Practical.
There is a big difference between a dreamer and a visionary. A dreamer has pie-in-the-sky ideas—thoughts that cannot be translated into any kind of relevant and reasonable solutions. A visionary, however, keeps both feet on the ground and devises ideas that can be implemented and are likely to find a waiting niche in the marketplace.

Not afraid to fail.
Vision itself can be scary, but the person of vision is not scared off by a monumental task or terrified by the prospect of an unsuccessful idea or activity. These people recognize that risk is part of the adventure of progress and that failure is but a steppingstone to perfection. Vision is analogous to accepting Christ as Savior; placing faith in Jesus is, by worldly standards,

a risk, but it is necessary before spiritual progress can be made. Our human frailties will not prevent us from reaching perfection, through Christ, as long as we are diligent in our efforts to know, love, and serve Him.

Driven to succeed.

While some church leaders would reject a forceful, success-oriented attitude, I believe that men of vision inevitably exhibit an unquenchable need to do their work as well as it can be done and to push the limits of what is possible. Far too often, church leaders are complacent and accepting of whatever happens or whatever can get done without much sweat. But look at societal visionaries and biblical figures who exemplified vision; they were zealous in their efforts to achieve their goals.

A team player.

Show me a man of vision who tries to do it all alone, and I will show you a person who will cause rather than solve problems. We have been created to live and work together, and being part of a unified team is a key element to success. The visionaries of the secular business world take great pride in surrounding themselves with the best available talent—people who are competent team players, but who are not necessarily cut out for the spotlight. The visionary has a lead role, but operates as part of the team. He cannot implement his vision by himself. The Lord Jesus is perhaps the greatest example of a person who had vision, but refused to do it all by Himself. Billy Graham is a man of vision whose crusades, publishing efforts, and other ministries are successful because of the strong team that has been developed and nurtured in concert with his vision.

A person of perseverance.

Vision is uncommon. As such, when shared or put into practice, it will generate resistance and may require unusual demands in terms of resources. A person who truly has vision, however, will not be deterred by hard times or new obstacles. Walt Disney had a vision for family entertainment, however, he failed seven times before his business finally caught on.

An expert in his field.
Men of vision tend to confine their vision to their areas of expertise. Few people with backgrounds in medicine make seminal contributions in management. People who have vast insight into manufacturing rarely make new and exciting things happen in education. A person of vision, therefore, first recognizes his area of expertise and then tries to make giant strides within that realm. Further, a person who lacks a true understanding of his arena is not likely to be centrally involved in ground-breaking progress in that field.

Unique Characteristics of Christian Visionaries
I believe two additional qualities distinguish Christian people of vision whose aim is to serve God through ministry.

Prayer.
I have yet to identify a Christian visionary for whom prayer was not a consistent, foundational reality. People to whom God has given the gift of vision pray for guidance, asking Him to open their eyes to opportunities and solutions. Their thirst for His direction is unmistakable. Embedded in their desire to serve is the constant request that He would see fit to use them as His instruments for blessing and that they would be keenly aware of their own strengths and limitations in fulfilling His ends.

Faith.
The second key to Christians who impact the world for God is that they have unshakable faith—both in God's sovereignty and in His desire for them to pursue their vision. Perseverance

without faith is folly. To truly know that the vision the individual seeks to implement is of God will get him through many difficult times without suffering losses due to self-doubt, worry, and self-reliance.

Can vision be developed? Not by our own will to do so. Vision is a quality God imparts to those for whom He has designed positions of significant leadership. However, while we cannot deign to accept vision in our lives, we can pray for Him to bestow it upon us.

Vision in Church Marketing

What, then, does vision look like in church marketing?

Let me suggest six steps that describe the way in which I have seen vision work well in evangelical churches.

First, a leader must possess the vision for his church. The leader does not have to be the pastor; he might be an elder or some other lay leader. That person would then work with the pastor to refine the vision so it can be defined for the body.

Second, the people of the church must be prepared to understand the vision. That is, they must comprehend the purpose of vision and how it shapes the life of the church. Sometimes a pastor shares his vision for the church and the congregation yawns its assent, figuring it sounds like an ambitious agenda for one man to implement. Since many Christians lack an understanding of what vision is and how it relates to the church, some training must precede the push to transform a spoken vision into an active vision. People must be conditioned for exposure to the vision—prepared to intellectually and emotionally process the information, and to actively embrace the course of action and purposes the vision represents.

Third, the vision must be articulated for the church. Advertising agencies have often said that having the best product in the marketplace is useless if consumers are not aware of it. Likewise, having a vision is of no value if the people who must make that vision happen are not informed of it.

Fourth, the people must accept the vision. If the church does not accept the vision, it certainly will not act in ways to make the vision a reality. I believe there are two reasons why people might reject a vision shared by their pastor.

In some cases, the people simply do not understand the vision. It might be the way in which the vision was communicated. It might be that the people are not ready for such a direction. The point is, the application of the vision might be premature. The church leaders, then, have the task of "retooling" the congregation for the parts they will play in the implementation of the vision.

In other cases, the vision is not suited to the reality of the congregation: right vision, wrong church. The pastor must assess whether or not he is in the right place to realize the vision. Sometimes the answer will be "no," requiring the pastor to make other provisions for carrying out the vision God has given him.

The fifth step is for the church, as a whole, to begin to make the vision a reality. Some individuals will have a more active role than others, but *everyone* in the body has a role in implementing the vision.

The final step is for the church to persevere. In almost every case with which I am familiar, a true vision from God requires stretching beyond what is normally considered to be reasonable. Pursuing the vision generally means attempting to do things that are neither easy nor typical. You may need to break new ground for ministry, and that will bring certain difficulties and hardships. Implementing the vision demands commitment and requires perseverance.

A Successful Example

Let me describe how one church was born from its pastor's vision. The pastor felt God's call to leave his existing church and start a new body in another area of the country. After considerable prayer, he was sure that he was being called to start a church unlike any that he had ever belonged to—much less pastored. He worked hard at thinking through the implications of his vision and making it practical. He eventually got to the point where he could articulate his vision verbally and in writing.

At that point, the pastor set about seeking people he could count as a core group—individuals who, upon hearing the vision, became excited about it and wanted to further explore how they could be a part of turning it into reality. The pastor continued his recruiting process, finding more people who were not interested in the vision than who were. However, by keeping the interested individuals involved in the growth of the church, the congregation that would eventually develop was certain to be built upon a unified vision.

Over a period of months, the core group took the necessary steps to fulfill the vision. Those with leadership capabilities began to design plans for different church projects and programs. Those who were capable helpers followed through on their tasks. Some people were not physical activists, but became prayer warriors for the fledgling church—consistently praying for God's provision for the needs of the church. In one year's time, that small core group managed to move the vision from a concept to a tangible organization. From its humble beginnings of meeting around the pastor's living room table for coffee and discussing a vision of what could be done in the community, the church grew to more than 1000 regular Sunday morning attenders in less than two years.

Was the vision's success due to the pastor's superb exposition of the Bible? No. Was it because the church grounds were attractive? No. Was it because the church was located in an area in which there were not enough churches to serve the population? No. (In fact, the thrust of the church was to reach those who were unchurched, not unhappily churched.) Very simply, this church was the result of the relentless pursuit of the vision the pastor possessed and articulated to his people. To this day, the church is growing. That growth is the result of the continual evaluation of every action the church takes in light of the church's vision.

The Relationship Between Vision and Marketing
What does vision have to do with marketing?

Earlier in the book, we described marketing as the series of activities that satisfies the goals and objectives of the producer and the needs of the consumer. Marketing, then, is the means by which both the consumer and producer can be satisfied. The vision is a representation of what the final outcome will be.

In the next chapter we'll discuss the next step in the church marketing process—planning goals and objectives. How can one reasonably develop goals and objectives without a vision?

Just in case you do not feel you have ever received an earth-shattering vision from the Lord of what your ministry will do to change the world, relax. Not everyone who has a successful ministry in progress has had that kind of experience—perhaps only a minority have. I cannot find any place in Scripture that suggests that everyone engaged in ministry will have a unique or world-changing vision.

It's no different in the secular marketing realm. I know of many companies where the company president did not have his own vision, but was so impressed by another corporate leader's vision that he adopted and adapted the other person's vision for his own use. In the same manner, I have worked with churches whose senior pastor described his vision for the church in terms of "having a community outreach like that of Pastor Smith, in Albuquerque."

The most important thing is to have a vision for your church that will work to the glory of God. Originality is not a requisite. Having the determination to see that vision become reality is.

6
Developing a Marketing Plan: The Importance of Planning

When my wife and I moved to California, we searched for a church that would be right for us. We searched and searched and searched. We were tired of churches that seemed like they had thrown everything together an hour before the service began. Our goal was to find a church where the worship and teaching was taken so seriously that preparation was evident, personal growth was possible, and commitment to service was appealing.

Several months and thirteen churches after our quest began, we wandered into the First Presbyterian Church of Hollywood. It was, by far, the largest church we had ever attended. However, we were struck by the professionalism and the sincerity of what was happening there.

It wasn't until sometime later, when we began to be more involved in the internal organization of the church, that I happened upon a notebook outlining each sermon that the senior pastor, Lloyd Ogilvie, was going to preach during the coming twelve months. Suddenly the light bulb in my brain flashed on! Here was a church that understood the importance of planning—a body that was freed from the tyranny of the urgent and fear of the unknown. The church's activities appeared well-planned because they were planned in advance with forethought and purpose.

Since then I have spent increasing amounts of time working with churches throughout the country. I have discovered that most successful churches operate in accordance with a ministry plan. That plan outlines the sermon topics and musical themes for each week, integrates special activities into the church calendar, coordinates church programing with budgetary realities, and the like. It represents a plan for how the church, as an organization, will behave. The underlying idea is that by thinking ahead, problems can be foreseen and avoided, and opportunities can be identified and taken advantage of to the greatest degree.

The Benefits of Planning

It may seem foolish to spend time talking about the benefits of planning. Indeed, many people are familiar with the expression, "Those who fail to plan, plan to fail." Unfortunately, mere intellectual assent to such a thought is quite different from putting it into practice. I am certain that most churches believe in planning, although relatively few actually do any meaningful planning. Most churches' response to planning is no different than the fact that nine out of ten Americans say they believe that Jesus Christ is the Son of God, but only three in ten have chosen to accept Him as Lord and Savior. In many cases, belief without commitment is self-deception.

Many churches that have an internal ministry plan have not considered the value of preparing a marketing plan. In some cases it is because they have not embraced the concept of marketing; in other cases it is because they have no idea how to go about preparing a marketing plan.

A marketing plan is simply a guidebook that includes the goals and objectives of a church, an assessment of current and future conditions, and a series of strategies and tactics for reaching the desired goals and objectives. In other words, the marketing plan is the blueprint for future activity that outlines how a church will get from where it is today to where it wants to be at a specific time in the future.

Hopefully, if you have gotten this far in the book, you are at least seriously considering the value of marketing for your church. So let's talk about the advantages of developing and implementing a marketing plan.

Here are five, briefly stated, important benefits that can be realized simply by conceiving a marketing plan for your church.

1. The plan is one way of identifying and clarifying the problems that prevent your church from growing and the opportunities that could be taken advantage of to enable growth to occur. Until you clearly understand your situation, there is no chance that your church will intelligently react to those opportunities.

2. A marketing plan gives "legs" to your vision. Without a guidebook on how to transform your dreams for the future into reality, chances are good that they will remain nothing more than dreams.

3. Confronting the problems and opportunities facing your church will force you to prioritize your ministry objectives. A key determinant in establishing the hierarchy of activities is your assessment of the church's strengths, weaknesses, and resources. If a detailed marketing plan does nothing else, it will make you recognize realistically what your church can and cannot accomplish. This, in itself, may serve as a catalyst to

motivate some people to action.

4. Your resources can be maximized by having a well-conceived strategy for the deployment of those resources. Waste can be reduced if the church's total needs are identified and the limited resources available are allocated for the greatest possible impact.

5. Responsibility and accountability can be realized through planning. Tasks are assigned, and people can be held accountable for their assignments according to predetermined timetables. More than identifying "who's at fault," however, the benefit of such accountability is that the church, if managed properly, can determine potential problems and short-circuit the difficulty before the solution itself becomes a problem.

Writing a Marketing Plan

Americans plan all the time. Housewives plan their shopping trips and perhaps even their purchases at the grocery store. Why? To use their time and resources more efficiently. Teachers plan their lessons in advance so they will have adequate time to cover the necessary topics and give students a sense of direction in their education.

The theory behind marketing planning is no different than that which motivates the housewife or teacher. By looking ahead, you can develop a plan that will enable you to market your church more efficiently and enhance your chances of reaching your goals.

The planning process is simple. If you are to follow the steps outlined in this section of the book, you should have already conducted your research to determine the needs, problems, and opportunities for your church. You should have conceived a vision for ministry based on that information. The next logical step is to think through how to turn your vision for marketing your church into reality. The result of that process will be your marketing plan—a written document that outlines where you are, where you want to be in the future, and how you are going to get there given your desires, your understanding of conditions, and your resources.

You do not need a doctoral degree in business management to develop a marketing plan. It is simply a matter of articulating your goals and objectives and the strategies and tactics you plan to employ to satisfy your desired ends. In fact, you may already be operating with some degree of marketing planning, by having bits and pieces of a formal strategy or by relying on a long-term concept of how to accomplish your goals for church growth and development that you've been keeping in your mind.

The marketing plan is one of a marketing-oriented organization's most basic and essential tools. Just as a pilot needs a flight plan, a bus driver requires a road map, or an orchestra needs a musical score to follow, a marketer has to have a document that outlines the actions needed to reach the goals set forth for the organization. The marketing plan is that document.

The first step in developing your marketing plan is to restate the mission of the church. All the marketing activity described in the plan must be consistent with the church's ministry purposes. It is helpful to put the church's mission in writing so there is never a doubt as to the body's underlying motives or intentions. By stating the purposes of the church up front and on paper, it is easier for those involved in the marketing plan's development and implementation to maintain a clear focus on ministry. The statement provides a standard against which every concept and approach can be tested to be certain that activities undertaken by the church are consistent with what the church is all about and what it is trying to achieve for Christ's Kingdom.

The next step is to recount what you learned about your

community and congregation through your research. As concisely as possible, articulate the fruits of your information collection phase in the second section of the marketing plan. Describe all the pertinent facts that will impact your plans and activities. This includes demographic information, data on local churches, and information about attitudes toward religion, Christianity, and even your church. A discussion of the prevailing needs of the population might be included. You could also include a short summary of key facts about your church's condition during the past several years: membership figures, budget figures, worship service attendance figures, Sunday school data, and so on.

Remember, the purpose of this section is to provide a factual base for the plans you are going to recommend for the church. If there is no empirical evidence to suggest that specific steps should be taken on behalf of the church, then there is no reason why the church leaders and laity should accept a plan that recommends such activities. The body of information that is provided should help portray the need for specific marketing activities or justify the decision to avoid certain efforts.

All of your factual discoveries are of limited benefit, however, unless they are translated into specific problems and opportunities that the church must confront. What trends in attitudes and behavior will affect your ability to minister? What limitations plague the church and will therefore prevent you from having an effective ministry in certain areas? What dominant needs of people in the community and congregation is the church well-positioned to address? Identify and describe—succinctly, but with sufficient detail to communicate the importance of the problem or opportunity—exactly what the condition is and how it relates to your church and its capabilities.

What is a marketing problem? It is a situation that needs

correcting. From the perspective of your church, a typical problem you are facing may be that few people are aware your church exists. Alternatively, your problem might be that in a town of 50,000 people, only fifty to seventy-five of them attend your church's worship services on a typical Sunday. Or, perhaps average attendance at your church is declining. The problem may be that your church has no meaningful outreach to the surrounding community, no sense of need for an evangelism program or thrust. You may be handcuffed by inadequate personnel or facilities, or perhaps a poorly executed service. The people who visit the church may leave feeling snubbed or rejected. The potential problems are infinite. The marketing plan should identify those that are most significant in the church's life and welfare.

A marketing opportunity, on the other hand, is a situation or condition that can be exploited for the benefit of the organization. By capitalizing on that condition, the church could gain ground toward reaching its objectives. For example, opportunities might grow out of special gifts and talents represented within the church. As people's lifestyles change, or as new people move into the community, obvious opportunities for church growth result. If unplanned resources become available, new avenues for growth and development open. Changes in community infrastructure—new roads, relocation of major employers, construction of new facilities—may provide changes for outreach. Additions to the church staff may facilitate certain types of ministry that previously were not possible.

To make things easier, prepare two separate lists of the problems and opportunities facing the church. First, list the problems in order of priority from most critical to least critical. Then do the same for the opportunities, starting with the most potentially beneficial or exploitable opportunity and ending with the least beneficial option.

Developing Marketing Objectives

Now is the point at which your vision is incorporated into the marketing process. Realize that your vision, when translated into marketing objectives, should be defined in specific and measurable statements. Marketing objectives represent the desired solution to a problem facing the church or the expressed desire to exploit an opportunity. The identification of objectives is especially key for the church, since all marketing activity should be designed to fulfill the ends they address.

Recognize that there is a difference between an organizational goal and a marketing objective. The latter is a solution or an approach that gives a sense of direction or guidance. An objective should lead to a strategy, which, in turn, will enable the organization to reach specific goals. Objectives should be measurable and achievable. They should be consistent with the overall ministry purposes of the church and should stretch the church to reach beyond what it has achieved in the past.

I'm familiar with a church that is currently developing a marketing plan. It has assembled a committee of businessmen from within the church to work with the church staff to create a marketing plan. They are struggling with the reality of having two separate populations within the church: people who are under thirty-five years of age and those who are sixty-five or older. It is almost as if there are two separate congregations meeting in the same building.

The committee recognizes, based on the community and congregational surveys they have conducted, that a high percentage of adults in the thirty-five to sixty-five age category live in the community but do not attend any church. Since the church's own attendance has declined slightly over the past several years, part of the vision for ministry is to attract more people who are in the "lost generation." The committee believes that by making their church more open and appealing to people in the thirty-five to sixty-four age segment, they can facilitate church growth, enhance the wholeness of the church as a functioning body by learning from that vital segment's perspectives and experiences, and have a church that is more capable of understanding and ministering to everyone in the community.

In working through their marketing plan, the committee first acknowledged the church's goal of expanding the weekly church attendance by twenty percent within the coming twelve months. The committee then developed the objective of increasing the attendance of thirty-five to sixty-four year-old people by 100 individuals (average Sunday attendance) within the next twelve months. (Given the size of the church, that figure represents the majority of the growth needed to reach the goal.) The committee is still working on the strategy and tactics for realizing those standards.

Strategies and Tactics
Until there is a plan for action, goals and objectives—no matter how well researched and clearly defined—will remain unattainable dreams. The next portion of the marketing plan should outline specific courses of action that the church must take to satisfy its objectives. The description of a strategy and series of tactics helps provide tangible direction and increases the likelihood of using your resources most efficiently to achieve your goals.

Conceptually, the process of developing tactics is simple. Having already set forth what you want to see happen for your church (objectives), you will now assign the responsibilities and outline the mechanics of how your vision will be implemented. You will identify who will be involved in a specific element of marketing your church, what each person will be doing, when they will engage in the specific activities, how their efforts relate to the objectives and efforts of those who will be pursuing other marketing objectives, and which marketing tools and resources will be utilized to achieve the desired results.

Determining what specific courses of action will satisfy your objectives should be no easy task. This probably cannot be done overnight: It may take weeks, or even months, to create and fine tune a set of strategies that will move the church forward. The experience of various organizations indicates that the most effective method is a type of brainstorming approach. Rather than accepting the first reasonable strategy that comes to mind or is offered for acceptance, several potential strategies aimed at accomplishing the same end might be proposed, with the best eventually being chosen.

The importance of developing realistic strategies and tactics—the action steps—cannot be overestimated. Having a series of objectives without related action steps is like buying a frozen dinner but not owning an oven; you may understand your problem and have some of the resources to solve it, but without a plan for implementation, you're in no better shape than if you didn't have the resources.

I suggest that you begin your section on strategies and tactics by taking each objective, one at a time, and developing an action plan for that objective. Start by restating the objective. Then provide a detailed outline of how you and your church will meet the objective.

Some experts suggest that you need to incorporate two separate aspects to develop an action-oriented strategy. First, *specify your target market:* Who are you seeking to impact? This might require listing the demographics of the target audience, how they can be found in your market, and any other distinguishing characteristics that will focus your actions. Second, *outline your marketing mix.*

The term *marketing mix* refers to how you will blend your product, price, promotions, and place into a strategy for marketing success. In other words, if the objective is to increase church membership among people thirty-five to sixty-five years old, how will you change the product, price, promotions, and place of your church to make that objective happen? These matters need to be addressed for each objective, so that a comprehensive understanding of how to achieve the objective within the framework of good marketing can be realized.

When all is said and done, it behooves you to go through each of the strategies developed and be sure that they are internally consistent and externally realistic. Since several action steps will most likely take place simultaneously, you will want to determine whether or not each step is truly compatible with the objectives for which it was designed, as well as whether or not it can be achieved with your limited resources.

You should also reconsider each strategy in light of what you know to be the situation you wish to impact. For example, increasing awareness of your church by placing advertisements in local newspapers might be an unreasonable strategy if you are a small church in New York City, where even a miniscule ad placed with any meaningful degree of frequency would cost as much as the pastor's annual salary!

To make each strategy as useful as possible, try to incorporate a deadline, a series of performance control standards, and some discussion of how resources will be allocated to satisfy the objectives.

Recognize, too, that merely developing strategies is not enough. An individual must take responsibility for communicating them to the people who will be expected to implement the strategies. Someone must be responsible for monitoring the performance and coordinating the implementation activities. There must also be some provision for developing and implementing alternative courses of action should the environment change dramatically, or the chosen strategy prove to be flawed.

Budgeting

Unfortunately, marketing invariably requires some outlay of resources, often financial. Before any marketing program can be approved and implemented, the church must determine the cost of the recommended steps. This means that marketing activities must be included in the church budget. Thus, we are developing a marketing plan that initially talks about the problems and opportunities, then identifies the activities that should be undertaken to capitalize on those, and finally determines what it will cost to properly market the church.

In some churches, a budget has been set aside specifically for marketing activities. In other bodies, marketing activities are underwritten by specific departments, committees, or boards that pay for the efforts made on their behalf and under their jurisdiction.

There is no single, correct way to approach the budgeting consideration. It is imperative, though, that the financial needs associated with marketing be calculated and considered in the approval process. Realize that as the cost of a program or strategy becomes evident, it may need to be redefined or restricted if it is too high. This should not be seen as a failure in the planning process. The fact that the shortfall was caught before any commitments related to the strategy were made is a testimony that the planning process is working for the best interests of the church.

7
Tactics: The Importance of What You Do

Several years ago I conducted a research project for one of the major television evangelists. His organization had been caught in a downward financial spiral for a couple of years, and he decided that something dramatic had to be done.

His goal was to raise several million dollars from new funding sources within the next year. Part of his strategy was to produce a prime-time television special, with an entertainment format, aimed at attracting new donors. To reach the fundraising goal established, he and his advisers determined that a good tactic would be to offer people who watched the special a free book—written by the evangelist—as a way of capturing their names and addresses for future direct mail marketing.

What transpired was one of the more colossal failures I know of in Christian marketing. Although we tested the special before it aired and warned that it would be rejected by the audience (Christian as well as nonChristian), the evangelist insisted on airing the program. He aired it in nearly 200 markets around the country, spending millions of dollars purchasing air time in the prime time hours. In anticipation of the onslaught of book requests, he had 500,000 copies printed, awaiting shipment from his warehouse.

Our research conducted after the special underscored not just the failure of the special to generate an audience, but also the futility of relying on a faulty marketing tactic. The free book, which was supposed to generate marketing leads, was of absolutely no interest to people. They had watched the program for entertainment, not education. The tactic was ill-suited for accomplishing the marketing strategy's aims. The warehouse, last I heard, still had 495,000 copies of the book.

On the brighter side, I've had the chance to work with a church in Southern California that recently held its first service after nearly two years of planning and preparation. Before it held its first worship service, the pastor worked with his core group toward a simple goal: have an opening-day attendance of at least fifty people. To reach that goal, one of the strategies was to make people aware of the church's existence. One tactic employed to make that strategy a reality was to send a monthly mailing to every household within a two-mile radius of the church's meeting place. Rather than send a brochure about the church, though, the pastor chose to send a series of needs-oriented brochures developed by another Christian organization, which were imprinted with the church's logo and the pastor's name and phone number.

That particular tactic worked like a charm. When the pastor met people at neighborhood meetings and other community events, he found that people recognized his name, associated him with the brochures, and wanted to know more about his church. That gave him a chance to speak with them about the church without forcing the issue. People responded to the brochures, and the church exceeded the goal of having fifty people at the opening worship service.

That pastor understood the importance of proper tactics. Tactics are the specific action steps you take to get from your vision to the point of goal achievement. Tactics are the things you do to fulfill your strategies. You can have the best series of goals and most innovative and efficient marketing strategies in the world, but without the right tactics, you're doomed. Tactics are where the rubber meets the road. Having a strategy without understanding what to do to make that strategy come alive leaves you no better off than if you did not have a plan and series of strategies.

Traditional Tactics
The traditional approach of churches to gaining new members has been three-fold.

Home visitation.
Many churches have undertaken home visitation. The idea is to send one or two representatives to knock on the door of a household that does not attend the church and present a formal invitation to attend the church. In some communities, this approach is restricted to visiting the homes of new homeowners—those individuals who have just moved into the community.

Unfortunately, home visitation reaps little gain for the effort expended. What is missing is a personal connection. Yes, there is a human connection between the visitors knocking at the door and the homeowner. However, because there is no relationship or bond between those two parties before the meeting takes place, most homeowners see the interaction as a bothersome intrusion by religious zealots. There is little distinction in the minds of many people between what happens in those encounters and what the Jehovah's Witnesses and Mormons attempt to do when they knock on people's doors. Please do not misunderstand me. In some cases, this approach will generate a fair amount of new traffic on Sunday morning. But the payoff for such a substantial expenditure of resources is not equitable.

Passive media.
A second common approach is for the church leaders to use passive media (e.g., a sign on the church lawn, mentioning times of the services) and hope that people will give the church a try. The emphasis in these churches is on the sermon; they believe the preaching will be strong enough to cause people to return to the church and eventually become members.

Unfortunately, there is a missing link in this chain. People do not attend a church because they see a sign on the front lawn or because the building looks well maintained. This is like sending a rock band on a concert tour and expecting an audience to show up at the concert hall simply because there is a band playing.

Paid mass media.
A third widespread tactic is to rely on paid mass-media advertising to bring in people. Advertisements might be placed in local newspapers and in the telephone book.

The reality is, few people who are not already actively seeking a church home will be stimulated enough by a black and white ad of dubious quality and content to change their lifestyle and start attending church services. Church advertising is rarely motivational and has a limited ability to reach people frequently enough to have any psychological impact. Research consistently indicates that paid advertising for churches, unless professionally developed and placed, has virtually no impact.

With the changes in American culture over the past two decades, these approaches have no place in church marketing. Perhaps they worked well in the past. The important point to remember is that these tactics are of little or no value in marketing a church today.

Tactics That Work

I have seen churches try a vast array of tactics to build up the size of the congregation. Some tactics have worked wonders, some have failed miserably. But do not forget a key principle in church marketing: What works for one church in one community may not work for a different church in a different community. There are no formulas for guaranteed church growth. There are, however, several tactics that have worked well in enough churches, in enough disparate situations, that they bear consideration.

A common thread between all of the strategies that work is that they address people's needs. In a community of older adults without kids, youth programs will not be a hook. In towns where tradition is strong and lifestyles are not keeping pace with the fads and trends of the day, a contemporary worship service could well be a disaster. Tactics designed to attract people to your church must grow out of an understanding of the mentality and lifestyles of the community and target audience you wish to reach and serve.

So, what works?

Personal invitation.
The most effective means of getting people to experience what a church has to offer is having someone they know who belongs to the church simply invite them to try it. Call it whatever you wish—word-of-mouth, personal invitation, friendship evangelism—this is indisputably the most effective means of increasing the church rolls. Why? Because it builds upon an

established relationship, which means that the recommendation or invitation springs from a credible source. More often than not, if the person being invited has any interest in the church, the mere fact that the church has the endorsement of a trusted friend or associate is sufficient to cause "product trial."

It sounds easy, but the tough part is to instill in the members your vision of church growth and help them see that *they* are the actual marketers of the church. The lay members possess the ability to make the church grow. They must understand it is up to each of them to invite people to visit the church. This means that the church leadership has a challenge before it:

- To make sure people feel so satisfied with the church that members would feel comfortable recommending it to friends;
- To communicate the importance of members inviting friends;
- To encourage members to invite their friends, preparing the laity for such boldness;
- To prepare the church for how to treat visitors once they grace the church with their presence.

In marketing, it is recognized that creating a sale is only half the battle; the other half is involved with creating a repeat purchase. What good has been accomplished if a person tries the product once and never buys it again? Very little. Thus, reinforcement of the decision to try the product becomes critical. For the church, this might mean having members not merely invite their friends and associates, but also interact with them afterwards about the experience and continue to encourage those people to give the church a second, third, and another try. The reinforcement process is key to successful church marketing.

Does interpersonal invitation really work? Our national research on why people attend church suggests that there are two major reasons why people attend their current church: legacy and invitation. By legacy, I mean that they have grown up in the community and attended that church since their youth, or that it has been family tradition to attend a church of a specific denomination. The other reason, however, is one that we can incorporate into an active marketing strategy. Having an aggressive word-of-mouth campaign to build church attendance is inexpensive and easily developed. It has the added advantage of including every church member in the operation, thereby making the activity truly a family affair.

Let me share with you another major reason, beyond the perfect fit between the interest in growth and the emphasis of personal invitations on relationships, to explain why I am so enthusiastic about personal invitation as a growth tactic. A recent national survey we conducted among unchurched adults indicated that twenty-five percent would attend a church if a friend ever took the time or made the effort to invite them. That's one out of four adults. If the unchurched population in this country is roughly 60 to 70 million people (our best estimate), that means 15 to 18 million adults are waiting to be asked to go to church! That is more people than live in the entire nation of Belgium or of Holland. It's twice the population of New York City. It is a lot of people! More important, it is an easy-to-capture market of high potential yield.

Several other tactics have demonstrated the ability to work well, depending on the market, the population segment desired, and the quality with which each tactic is implemented.

Small group studies.
Small group studies have shown a great ability to both build the existing body and to easily incorporate outsiders into the flow of the church. These studies, which usually meet in the

home of one of the group members, might number eight to twelve people and appear to be most effective when they meet once a week. The purpose of the study is to develop a family unit, built around the Word of God, where everyone who comes has a common interest: the desire to know more about God.

There are many variations on what small groups do when they are together. The most common approach is a combination of Bible study, prayer, and personal sharing. Other activities undertaken by groups include an external missions focus (i.e., doing local missions or social action work), and praise and worship time (singing and communion).

The value of groups, once again, is the emphasis on building relationships. If properly led, these groups can have a tremendous evangelistic impact. It is interesting to read the works of Paul Cho, who has built his church in South Korea around small groups. His experience is not uncommon. The burden on the church, in this case, is to develop a structure for small groups and assist in the identification and training of small group leaders.

Program.
A programmatic approach would be for a church to place great emphasis on its children's programs. In some communities, this distinction alone would cause a church to have a major impact and grow quickly. (Note that the sentence said some, not all.) With baby boomers assuming parental roles, and given the lifestyles that so many of them lead, family is an increasingly important consideration. Nurturing children in spiritual matters is often seen as a key building block for youngsters, but the parents may feel incapable of providing such education. A church that shares their perspective on the importance of children and provides a quality program will stand a better chance of attracting a strong market share.

Again, it is critical to recognize that simply having a

program is of no intrinsic value. The American public is a discerning lot. We have come to expect quality in every product and service we encounter. Those that lack quality will be discarded because we believe we deserve the best, and because there are so many available options that we will eventually locate the best. If your church cannot provide an excellent program—whether it is a children's program, a men's program, the church service, or any other endeavor—you would do the Body of Christ a service by not offering the program at all.

High Risk Tactics
A variety of activities have worked very well in some communities and have absolutely bombed in others. These are tactics that might be considered high risk. You can win big or lose big, depending on how adequately they are executed, and how well they fit the needs of your target audience.

Media ministry.
Some churches have attempted to build their congregation through a media ministry. This might entail the pastor writing a column in the newspaper. It might mean buying time on the local radio station for a radio ministry, in which past sermons and lessons are aired. In some cases, congregations have gone so far as to videotape their church service and air it on local cable channels, hoping to build an audience of people who will eventually visit the church.

The radio and television approach, in particular, is of dubious value. The costs are usually high and the returns low. If free air time can be obtained, the costs can be reduced to those associated with production and promotion. Even those costs, however, can be considerable. The risk, then, is a trade-off between finances and visitors generated. Few local churches I have encountered have found the equation to work in their favor. The same outcome is true for the newspaper column approach, although there is less financial risk involved. The resource being wagered in that case is the time of the pastor. Conversations with a number of pastors who have gone this route also suggest that the yield is slight for the expenditure of time and effort.

Telemarketing.
One of the more ludicrous approaches that has recently become popular in some churches is telemarketing. The church will hire a telephone solicitation company (or may attempt to build its own team of telephone solicitors) to call every household in certain areas of the community and invite them to attend the church. This approach is plagued by the same weakness as the door-to-door invitation—there is no relationship on which credibility can be based—but is intensified by the lack of physical contact. This impersonal tactic works well for selling magazines and insurance policies, but not for a product that is based on relationships.

Direct mail.
Another recent tactic that has gained nationwide favor is direct mail marketing. In most communities it is possible to rent lists of residents, enabling the church to send brochures, letters, and other printed material to thousands of homes to invite people to attend the church. On a per household basis, the cost is relatively small, although the aggregate cost adds up quickly if the campaign is seeking to reach a large area or is using expensive materials.

I encountered one church that put out a mailing just before Easter—a good time to search for church visitors, since many people wander into churches during the traditional holy days of Easter and Christmas. Amazingly, not a single person from the 40,000 households reached by the mailing came to visit that church! This was an expensive lesson in direct marketing. On examining their materials, it seemed apparent to me why nobody showed up. Who wants to be told that they are sinners and will go to hell if they don't change their lifestyle? That's essentially what the brochure told people. The colors were drab, the message was one of fear and guilt, and the church was in a relatively inaccessible location. In this situation, the problem was not the medium, it was the message.

I have worked with other churches that sent out several tens of thousands of brochures—professional, well-crafted pieces of literature geared to addressing felt needs and making people feel welcome and as if they were in for a valuable, positive experience. These churches have seen several hundred new faces at the next Sunday service. Generally, the return rate—i.e., the percentage of households who respond to the mailing—does not exceed one percent. Thus, if you sent out 1,000 brochures, don't expect more than ten newcomers. Send out 10,000 pieces, and your response would be above average if more than 100 new people came.

Direct mail *can* work well for the church. However, with the average household now receiving in excess of 1,500 unsolicited pieces of mail per year, it takes a polished, professional piece to cut through the clutter and make such a significant impression that it will alter an established behavior pattern. If your mailing is done amateurishly, you will undoubtedly lose your shirt in the process. If it is handled professionally, you *might* emerge a winner.

Realize, too, that with direct mail, even more so than other tactics, the key to making the prospecting process work for you is to identify the visitors, gently reinforce their decision to attend, and graft them into the network of church relationships. Simply getting people to come through the doorway on a Sunday is not enough. If they are not made to become a part of a living and exciting organism, they will never walk through the doorway again.

Community events.

Sponsoring community events can also be used to introduce people to the church in a nonthreatening setting, giving visitors something of value the very first time they come in contact with the church. The ability to transfer any newly generated interest in the church and goodwill resulting from the event into the next step—a visit to the church when it is doing its spiritual activities—is as important as how the event itself is managed. However, since people are taking cues from the event, if the nature of the event, the way in which it is coordinated and promoted, and the perceived quality are not up to expectations, the church can do itself more harm than good.

One church that has used the community event process to great advantage is North Coast Presbyterian Church (NCPC) in California. It has begun an annual series of events called KidsFest, in which several weekends are devoted to serving the needs of children in the community. The church has utilized the events as an opportunity to gain community exposure, and to position itself as being in touch with the interests of youngsters and capable of putting together a well-fashioned program of events that will help parents nurture their children.

NCPC has maximized the events by enlisting other community organizations and businesses as cosponsors. They have had Burger King, Domino's Pizza, and local restaurants donate food and drinks. They have had athletes from San Diego's professional sports teams put on clinics. Nonprofit organizations such as Mothers Against Drunk Driving have joined the church in sponsoring the events. The local media have provided wide coverage, giving NCPC literally tens of thousands of dollars of media time and space. And that media coverage has both a level of credibility that advertising could not hope to achieve and a far greater audience reach.

The caution, though, is that putting together such meaningful events is very hard work and takes many months of planning and effort. It also requires a keen understanding of what matters to people in your community and knowing how to sponsor an event that will capture the fancy of the population, without smacking of religion. NCPC had many adults visit the church because they were impressed by the professionalism of the events and the fact that the church cared about more than theology. There were no sermons at the events, no pleas for people to attend NCPC forthwith. But do not underestimate the difficulty involved in turning a community event into a harvesting activity.

Developing Tactics
Unfortunately, there is no magic formula for developing viable tactics. However, there are a few considerations that can make the procedure more likely to succeed.

First, always refer back to your research about community needs. If you can determine what people are looking for, or what opportunities exist for marketing solutions, you stand a better chance of developing courses of action that will find acceptance in the marketplace.

Second, do as much secondary research as you can to figure out what church marketing tactics have been tried in your area and what has worked and what has failed. If another church has recently found out that direct mail does not draw visitors in your community, and if you are convinced they ran a good direct mail campaign, there's no virtue in trying to learn the same lesson on your own. Conversely, if another church has found that a community event is what people in your community respond to, perhaps such an approach bears further investigation.

Third, it is to your advantage to test any tactic before going with that tactic full speed ahead. If it is a direct mail campaign, send the mailing to a sample of households and find out what kind of response it generates. If telemarketing is your tactic, try it with a handful of households and find out what kind of reactions people have to the script, the approach, and the product. Before investing a large pool of your precious resources in an untried commodity, do whatever you can to evaluate the tactic.

Fourth, do not restrain the creative juices of your core group. When developing tactics, a few off-the-wall suggestions will be made. On occasion, they are only off-the-wall because they are novel. Yet some of those novel concepts can work wonders. Think about it. Many of the fastest growing companies in the nation are based on novel tactics. Domino's Pizza is based on a unique tactic (quick delivery of the product). The California Raisin Advisory Board used a unique executional element (a form of tactics) in devising the "dancing raisins" television commercial that has led to unanticipated sales growth.

Finally, make a realistic assessment of your resources before agreeing to any tactic. If you do not have the resources to pull it off, drop that tactic. You will be better off neglecting an attractive tactic that you could not do justice to, than starting a course of action and having to dump it in midstream.

8
Marshaling and Utilizing Resources: The Importance of Implementation

Several months after I started our company, I had the opportunity to help a major publishing company develop a marketing plan. For me, the prospect was exciting: having a chance to shape the future direction of a sleeping giant, a company that had tremendous resources and potential but lacked a sense of direction and how to best utilize its wealth of resources.

For three months I worked with the team assembled by the publisher. In the end, we had what seemed to be a well-conceived, realistic, workable plan for growth and development. The publisher's marketing team was pleased with their accomplishment and proudly presented the plan to their management.

Today, several years later, that publishing firm is in the same state of disarray and paralysis that characterized it when we first set out to provide some direction. I truly believe that the problem was not with the plans—if they were far off the mark, they could very simply have been modified. The problem was that once the plan was presented, after everyone nodded their approval of the concept of planning and the idea of waking up the company to realize its true potential, the report sat on a shelf. Nobody ever took ownership of the plan and dedicated himself to making the plan happen.

The lesson I learned was that the marketing process doesn't end once a good marketing plan has been developed. The countless hours and amount of energy that go into carefully conceiving, revising, and fine tuning the plan are wasted unless there is a serious commitment within the organization to implement the plan. The fact that the publisher developed the plan was, as far as I can tell, just another example of why the organization was dormant: the inability to act on good ideas and plans, which relegated the company to a slow, painful, and unnecessary decline.

The plight of that publisher is similar to what happens in the average evangelical church on Sunday. A challenging, convicting sermon may be preached. People in the congregation listen to the exhortation, nod in assent, then leave the church grounds and continue their lives without any change in attitude or behavior. This pattern is frustrating for the preacher and a wasted opportunity for personal growth by members of the congregation.

Unless you have thought about and developed a way to ensure that your marketing plan is more than just a document that will gain people's intellectual assent before it resides permanently on a shelf in the pastor's den, there is a high probability that your marketing plan will become just another wasted resource.

I believe a church can take seven steps to prepare the way for the successful implementation of the marketing plan.

Those steps, in order of enactment, are listed here:

- Establishing one person as the marketing director for the church;
- Creating ownership of the plan among the key leaders of the church;
- Identifying the resources and conditions needed to move ahead with the plan;
- Identifying specific resources that can be used in the plan's implementation;
- Training leaders in the basics of marketing, to maximize their input and their talents;
- Holding people accountable for doing their assignments;
- Implementing the entire plan.

While there are never any guarantees of success, experience has shown that organizations have a greater chance of success if they do follow the path laid out in their plan.

A Marketing Director
Marketing has little to do with titles and organizational turf. It has much to do with ideas, action, and responsibility. The idea of choosing a marketing director is not so much to develop a new personnel structure or a staff position within the church, as it is to ensure that the marketing plan will not fail due to lack of leadership. A title, such as marketing director, is not necessary. What *is* necessary is that an individual is chosen to guide the plan from the report stage through the action stage.

The idea of selecting a single adult to spearhead the marketing process will, in itself, buck the tide in many churches. The average church in the United States has one of two styles of management. There is the "strong pastor" congregation, in which all that happens is a consequence of the will and force of the pastor. Whatever gets put into practice is due to his determination to make those events transpire. There may or may not be committees and boards established and operating. In reality, if those groups exist; they are mere figurehead entities, existing to make the church look good, or because the church's bylaws or denominational regulations require such groups.

The second typical situation is where the church is ruled by one or more committees or boards. This is leadership by committee, and often is typified by an excruciatingly slow and labored decision-making process. This type of church is often incapable of reacting quickly to an opportunity or problem because power is vested in a group that meets infrequently. Further, it is less common for such churches to embrace a new program with zeal, because the vision must be equally shared by every member of the group that will be responsible for supporting that activity. It is a case of a chain being as strong as its weakest link. Too often, church boards are restrained by having too many weak links.

If the marketing plan is to have a chance for successful implementation, it is best to have a single individual take control of it and have the authority to do whatever needs to be done (within reason) to make things happen according to schedule. When committees and boards become involved in implementation, momentum is frequently lost by the deliberate speed with which the ship pitches forth (if any momentum can be established in the first place). The best scenario is to have the appropriate groups give their blessing to both the plan and the specific individual who will be held accountable for the marketing process. Recognize that this is how successful corporations operate their businesses. They are run by a board of directors who give their approval to a plan, and then expect an executive to turn the plan into an operational system. The church, as a business, should emulate that procedure.

A significant advantage of having an individual assume leadership of the marketing program is the ability of the person to maintain an aggregate and flexible perspective on what happens related to the church. The individual can manage the marketing activities more efficiently because he will have a sense of the big picture—an understanding of what the end result should look like. As events change and impact the nature of the plans originally devised, alterations can be made to keep the plan viable and realistic. There is the ability to respond logically and quickly without rupturing the underlying foundations and purposes for which the plan was conceived.

Understand, too, that candidates for the marketing director are often taken from the limited pool of individuals who played an active role in the development of the plan itself. Who could better understand, sell, and oversee a plan than a person who played an integral part in the birth and refinement of that plan?

Please avoid the mistake that many churches make: assigning the marketing leadership role to the pastor. This assignment should not automatically be given to the pastor. Even in a church where things happen almost exclusively as a result of the pastor's strength of character and will, a marketing plan may not receive the attention and consideration it needs from someone who is already bogged down in daily church operations.

In very small churches, by virtue of the fact that there are no others who are capable of managing the process or who have fully accepted the vision, the pastor may wind up as the *de facto* marketing director. However, a church should do its best to select the strongest possible candidate for marketing leadership within the church. That may mean someone other than the pastor—someone with marketing experience, marketing training, a flair for marketing, and the time to properly manage the process.

Ownership

The marketing director's first true test will be his or her ability to develop widespread ownership of the marketing plan and process among the church members, for their involvement will make a difference in the marketing of the church.

In management and marketing, ownership is a critical concept. It implies that a person does not simply allow ideas and principles to be discussed and just give intellectual assent to a course of action. A person who owns the plan is one who actually takes a measure of responsibility for it—it belongs to him, and he realizes that the fate of the plan is in his hands. Because he has assumed ownership, any failure of the plan to be implemented is a personal failing. Conversely, when the plan is put into practice and makes a difference in ministry, it is seen as a personal victory, a consequence of that person's commitment and diligence.

How does ownership occur? Let's use Bill, an elder in a church that has just prepared a marketing plan, as our example. Bill first has to recognize that the church is in a situation in which a marketing plan is needed. He has to accept the fact that marketing is a proper activity for the church to engage in, and that marketing is a solution (either full or partial) to the church's present condition. He must agree that all is not well with his church and that things could be improved. The need may not be a matter of pressing problems that plague the church so much as the recognition that ministry opportunities are not being exploited to their fullest potential. Bill must acknowledge that his church could be in a better situation and could accomplish more for God's Kingdom.

It is not enough for Bill to see the church's need. He must also accept the fact that the marketing plan represents a solution to the need. He has to see the plan, hear it described, and buy into the approach. Bill has to clearly see the vision for what the church could become and view the marketing plan as the tangible bridge between that vision and a future reality.

Much like a senator who votes to accept or reject a piece of legislation, Bill has to go on record, indicating that he understands what the marketing plan is endeavoring to do and affirms its goals, objectives, strategies, and tactics. In the same way that baptism is a public statement of acceptance of Christ, Bill's acceptance of the marketing plan is a public statement to other leaders and church members. Bill must indicate that he understands the content of the plan and concurs that the church ought to do what it can to put the steps set forth in the plan into action.

Up to this point, Bill has only a limited, personal investment in the marketing plan. He has heard it, read it, and acknowledges that it would be good medicine for his church. His support is intellectual: so far it is an arms-length, limited-risk support. This is an important and necessary precursor to the most important step. But the most critical step is for Bill to personally accept responsibility for the implementation. He must invest himself in it, just as he would invest his hard-earned salary into the stock market or a home. If Bill reads the document, nods his approval, and walks away without a personal commitment to doing something about it, little has been gained. It is imperative that Bill, as a church leader, not only see the value of the marketing plan but support it 100 percent. He has to *own* the plan.

Ownership means that Bill has to accept the fact that he is accountable for his actions relative to the implementation process. If the plan fails, he is partly responsible for that failure. It is in Bill's best interests, as well as those of the church, to put his full energy behind the plan to ensure that it does, in fact, enhance the standing of his church. Because it is Bill's church, and he is a leader in and member of that church, he has a vested interest in the plan's success.

Is it necessary for every lay leader in the church to own the marketing plan? No. That is not only unnecessary, but unrealistic. Certainly, it would be best if every leader in the church owned the plan; the strength found in unity is undeniable. However, few churches find total harmony in any operational activities. The marketing director should seek to gain the approval and involvement of all, but not be discouraged or thwarted by his inability to do so. A significant marketing process can occur with even a few people who understand the plan and are committed to making it happen.

Recognize, though, that a central role of the marketing director is to build a team of people who will share the load of making the marketing plan work. Just as it is unwise to place the brunt of the marketing effort on the pastor's shoulders, it is unwise to expect the marketing director to represent the totality of the marketing department. The director should see his role as building a team of helpers who will work with him to see that the vision becomes a reality.

Identifying Potential Resources

Once a group of members has agreed to put their support and energy behind the plan, it is time to identify both the resources needed to implement the plan and their sources.

Some churches might have the marketing director pencil out all of the resources that ideally are needed to make the plan happen, but there is value in having the central players on the marketing team get together and share their ideas on what resources will be necessary. Not only will this approach help solidify their understanding of the vision underlying the plan and their sense of teamwork, but it may expand the horizons of the resource base that will be sought for the project. This group effort may have the additional benefit of sparking ideas about where to find the needed resources for the needs identified by the group.

When the time comes to identify the necessary resources,

there should be an exploration of both internal and external resources—that is, resources that are within and outside the church. Many churches limit their prospects for success by assuming that they must have every needed resource within the church. This is neither realistic nor desirable, since it puts false limitations on the church's ability to reach out and minister most effectively.

Four types of resources are especially useful to identify. The plan is not going to get anywhere unless you identify the human resources that are required to make the plan happen. You will need people to volunteer to do various aspects of the marketing. This could entail people to make telephone calls, people to write press releases, people to type reports or documents, and people assigned to other tasks. You will need people to list useful contacts for the church and individuals who have skills and talents that could be utilized in moving the church toward its goals. Some people may be brought in as teachers, offering training in areas in which the church is weak. Other people may simply be fountains of information and knowledge, who simply offer wisdom and data that will prove useful in the decision making that inevitably occurs.

Facilities must be established for the marketing plan. This may entail access to rooms for meetings. It might involve the use of equipment, such as copiers, computers, or postage meters.

A third necessary element is other tangible but expendable materials, such as paper and envelopes.

Last, but not least, is the need for money. Marketing does require cash to make things happen. How much money is needed depends on how ambitious the plan is and the way in which the planners develop the marketing activities.

Where are these resources to be found? Most of them already exist within the church budget, offices, and congregation. Few churches have consciously inventoried the skills, abilities, and resources of the congregation. To some people, this may smack of personal exploitation. However, the purpose is not to take unfair advantage of whatever an individual has to offer, but to truly treat the church body as a family. In a family, there are no qualms about asking another family member to chip in and do his or her share of a task. If a person is a member of your church body, you should not shy away from asking for help simply because American society considers that a forward approach. If we do not ask for the help of our brothers and sisters, the chances are we will not receive such help.

Many external sources of assistance can be utilized, too. Teaching, training, and consultation in specific areas of marketing, communications, and finance might be gained by seeking help from parachurch organizations, from faculty at Christian secondary schools and colleges, and from denominations. Government agencies sometimes provide useful resources to community organizations, ranging from guest speakers to research reports. Financial needs might be partially covered by grants and endowments from foundations or wealthy individuals.

The purpose of pooling resources before getting deeply involved in the plan's implementation is to notice weaknesses (either in the plan or in the ability to implement it) before it is too late, and to gain a better sense of how to most efficiently allocate what is inevitably a limited pool of resources. With proper planning, the resource pool can be stretched to better satisfy needs than might otherwise have been accomplished.

Training Leaders
The church is not meant to provide an MBA for every person who expresses interest or willingness to help the church in its marketing adventures. However, the church would best serve itself by providing the most integrally involved people with some modicum of training related to the areas in which they will be involved.

Realistically, this will be a short, rather cursory, look at the marketing process. Four resources can be used to provide a fuller understanding of the marketing perspective. The most common is to have each person read material about marketing's purposes, process, and benefits. (Chapter eleven contains a list of the books and articles that might be used for this purpose.) Audio tapes are an alternative, as are videotapes. It is also feasible to attend a seminar on marketing or to have a specialist come to your church and provide a private session on marketing and how it pertains to the church.

Frankly, my experience has been that providing some type of training or perspective is most effective when it is done as a group process. Everyone could be given a book to read, and the group could convene two weeks later to discuss the main principles and how they relate to what the church is striving to achieve. If people are given a book and left on their own, chances are they will not read the material, nor will they think through the church's marketing process. Providing a group training context gives a greater incentive to take the assignment seriously, and the group discussion enables everyone to become involved.

Once again, it is important that the group leader be well-prepared and capable of putting it all in perspective. The role of discussion leader might best be played by an outsider, perhaps a marketing professor or marketing director from a parachurch organization, who can come in and lead the group down an identified path.

This step may appear to be overkill; for your church, perhaps it is. Consider, however, the value of having everyone who will be involved in the church's marketing in a leadership role start with the same vision of the results desired and the same understanding of how the marketing process works. The ability to provide your key people with this more comprehensive perspective is a benefit.

Accountability

One of the key tasks of leadership is to hold people accountable for their responsibilities. This is especially critical in church marketing. The team members are working as volunteers, trying to fit their own efforts into what may already be a full schedule of daily duties. Nevertheless, if the marketing plan is to see the light of day and make inroads for the church, everyone who gets involved must be counted on to uphold their end of the agreement. The marketing director's role is to be sure that people do what they pledged to do.

Naturally, this has to be handled with grace and sensitivity. Remembering that the purpose of the aggregate marketing effort is to build the church—not tear it apart by creating new tension and dissension—the director must be firm, but flexible and loving. Expectations have to be clearly established with each person before he or she accepts a task, and the director has to remain aware of how well the job is being done. If people do not live up to their end of the agreement, they must be told so, in a gentle, but dispassionately clear way.

The director must also realize that if some people fail to live up to their promises, the slack must be picked up in some other way. Accountability in the marketing program is not put in place simply to teach brothers and sisters a biblical principle, but to enhance the probability of the marketing plan realizing its full potential.

Implementing the Entire Plan

I have seen organizations progress midway through the implementation phase and fade out, leaving the other half of their plan in limbo. This is like building half a bridge. Everyone is worse off for the effort because resources have been expended, yet the project is only half completed and, therefore, unusable. If you are going to start implementing the plan, finish the job. (Read Luke 14:28 for additional motivation!)

Remember, implementing the entire plan does not mean that modifications cannot be made once things are underway. As effort is put forth and conditions change in response to the implementation, it is likely that changes in the original plan must be made. However, alterations are very different from jumping ship once the process has begun. To reach the desired ends, the director may assume the position of cheerleader, encouraging his team to persevere through unforeseen difficulties, and rejoicing in the victories that they earn.

Magnitude of Effort

In reading this and the previous chapter, you may be struck with a sinking feeling, thinking that this marketing stuff takes more energy and effort than your church could possibly muster. Please realize that the amount of time and other resources required to fulfill a marketing plan depends solely on the magnitude of the goals in your plan. If you are seeking to radically overhaul your church in one major marketing push, chances are your feeling is right—you may be biting off more than you can handle. If, however, you look at marketing as a process that is never completely finished, but is constantly evolving in response to past efforts, new conditions, a changing pool of resources, and a perpetually refined vision of what the church can be, then perhaps the magnitude of the marketing effort becomes more manageable.

It is in the best interest of your church to set a series of realistic goals within a reasonable time frame. If this is done, your chances for having a successful marketing experience—and, therefore, a continuing marketing program—will be significantly higher.

9
Communicating with the Public: The Importance of Your Message

C urrently I am working with a large mainline church that suffers from the inability to communicate. Here is a church with a large and growing faction of baby boomers, located in a dynamic metropolitan area, that bears all the marks of tremendous ministry potential. But that body has little hope of leaving a positive mark on the community until its communication channels and processes are dramatically improved.

Why can't the church thrive? Very simply, it has failed to communicate its vision to the congregation, thereby leaving the church with a team composed of all chiefs and no Indians. The church has failed to convey an image of being relevant and caring to the people who are on the outside looking in—those who are curious, but are neither converted nor committed. Consequently, it has rendered itself incapable of effectively reaching those people. The church has also failed to communicate what it stands for and how it plans to reach the community. Because of that, the leaders of the community have written off the church as a dead body—a church of little consequence or potential.

The sad part is that the church has earnestly been working to develop plans and strategies for becoming an aggressive and significant servant of the Lord. The church leaders are learning the hard way that by keeping their vision and plans a virtual secret, they have sealed the fate of the church. Unless they clearly and persuasively communicate their intentions to the world in which the church operates, that body will stagnate and eventually decline.

Let's not be unduly harsh on this church, however. It is but one carrier of the disease that afflicts thousands of evangelical churches in this country. Communication, though a common process, is an inordinately complex and demanding undertaking. Yet, mastering that difficult process represents a key to church growth.

Why is communication so vitally important to the health and vitality of the local church? Communication is the means by which we reach our ministry goals. You cannot find a healthy, growing church that is plagued by ineffective communications. Such an animal simply does not exist. If your church is going to maximize its potential, it is imperative that you understand the communication process and constantly strive to upgrade how well you and others in your church communicate.

Two Kinds of Communication

To understand communication, we have to recognize that the process can be evaluated in several ways. First, let's understand the difference between mass and interpersonal communication. Mass communication is when a message is sent to a large audience simultaneously. There is no direct or immediate interaction with the audience in the mass process. In contrast, interpersonal communication is used in situations in which the message is directly and personally conveyed from one person to another. This approach provides the opportunity for a spontaneous response by the receiver of the message—a luxury that is not possible in the mass communication scenario.

Research indicates that interpersonal communication is most efficient and more likely to stimulate a personal response. Mass communication, on the other hand, boasts a broader reach and the possibility of generating a response from a greater number, although it is likely to be less emotionally intense.

Regardless of the approach, communication exists to inform or persuade an audience. In the marketing process, then, communication is important to reap the benefits of both informing and persuading. Informing people about conditions and alternatives is a central element in stimulating a response. Communication is also the means to influence people's behavior relative to the product, price, and distribution network. Without communication, marketing would be a strictly intellectual activity, lacking any semblance of practical utility and void of any widespread participation and involvement.

Goals of Communication

As alluded to in the example of the church that has kept its abilities, plans, and strategies a hidden treasure, church communications fulfill three primary roles.

First, it is imperative that the church communicate with its members. The congregation has to receive a concise vision statement, the plans and strategies by which the leaders hope the church will realize the vision, and the responsibilities that befall each member. Unless these aspects are conveyed to the congregation, one of two things will likely happen: the entire brunt of the marketing effort will fall on the shoulders of the few who developed the marketing plans and strategies, or the marketing effort will evaporate altogether due to lack of support (psychological, physical, financial, and spiritual).

Second, the people from outside the church who visit or evaluate it from afar must be informed of what the church is all about. Every organization emits an image—an impression of what the organization is like and what it is all about. Your church should think about the image it presently gives to outsiders, since that image will impact your ability to minister to those outside the church. Beyond the image, though, your church should be communicating a warmth of heart and soul to outsiders in tangible ways, such as by inviting them to be part of your church community.

Third, your communications should tell other organizations what you are about and what you are accomplishing. This is part of your organizational positioning. To have the greatest impact possible, your church should be recognized by other organizations as a cog in the community structure—just as necessary and vital to the community's health and growth as the police department, supermarkets, schools, and other businesses. It is interesting to listen to local leaders talk to visitors about the strengths of their community. Often, they speak in terms of economic forces, governing structures, and other people-building entities and opportunities. It is unusual for leaders to mention the value added to the community by one or more of its churches. This is largely because churches have failed to communicate their goals and accomplishments to the world around them.

Steps Toward Effective Communication
Regardless of the audience with which you are trying to communicate, or the nature of the message you wish to convey, the basic principles of communication remain the same.

As in the development of the marketing plan, the communication process begins with a sense of the objectives you seek to fulfill. The most common communication objectives are to either raise people's awareness levels, motivate people to action, help people understand something, or change existing attitudes. Depending on the particular objectives you wish to meet, your approach to communicating with the target audience will be quite different.

After determining your objective, you can develop the specific messages that will enable you to achieve your objectives. There are several communication strategies or styles from which to choose, and as the communicator, it is your responsibility to select the strategy that best fits your objectives.

One strategy is to give the audience a rational message. In this approach you offer information, using data and logic to either inform or persuade. If your objective is to enhance people's awareness of a condition or help them comprehend a situation, providing a rational message may be very effective. If, however, you seek to rally people to action, or to alter a basic attitude, this type of message may have only limited impact.

A second strategy is to use an emotional message. The goal of this approach is to touch the receiver through his other emotions. In church ministry, the emotions we have traditionally stimulated most through our communications have been fear, guilt, love, and joy. By attempting to reach people emotionally, the aim is to create a behavioral response that grows out of the intensity of the emotional energy that has been stirred. It would not be efficient to use emotional messages simply to heighten awareness or comprehension. Emotional messages are most useful for creating an active response.

Providing a moral message is yet another strategy. This type of message appeals to a person's sense of right or wrong. Perhaps more than the other avenues of communication, moral-based messages must strike a balance between sensitivity and self-righteousness. Moralistic messages are most effective for inciting an active response. Using this approach to create awareness or comprehension rarely reaps an adequate payback.

Reward-based communications are intended to convince the receiver that he or she will accrue personal benefit from a specific reaction. Messages that offer rewards, either tangible or intangible, can be particularly effective for grasping people's attention. Much of today's product advertising is reward based, largely in response to the "me-ism" that permeates our society. Reward-based messages can best be used to garner awareness, active response, and attitude change. However, when using this approach, you must ensure that the reward will, in fact, be delivered once the prescribed action is undertaken. The church, in general, has often failed to recognize this critical point. Thus it attracts people through the promise of specific rewards (such as meaningful friendships, relevant sermons, providing a sense of personal peace), only to anger many seekers by failing to make good on those promises.

Finally, there are also messages that are geared to perceptual change. A person rarely enters a situation without a set of preconceived notions. Sometimes those notions are based on facts, sometimes they are not. The goal of perceptual-change messages is to shift existing attitudes, beliefs, opinions, or values to a position that is more compatible with that of the message sender.

As a communicator, then, you should understand what your desired end result of communication is, and what type of message is best suited for exacting that response from your audience. You should also conceive a strategy for communicating your message as a part of your process of selecting the optimal type of message. This means articulating, for yourself, who you seek to reach with the message, what medium you will use for that purpose, the content of the message, and some of the obstacles you will face in achieving a successful interaction.

Churches generally overlook this last consideration. We blithely assume that if we say something, our audience will hear it completely and interpret it the way in which we intended. How naive! In common, everyday communications, we run into many examples of messages that are distorted somewhere in the chain of communication. Even if the distortion is not due to unclear communication from us, we nevertheless bear the consequences of that breakdown. It is to our advantage, then, to think through what the barriers, obstacles, and points of fuzziness might be, and to structure our communication to avoid or address those weak spots.

Problems of Distorted Communication

Let me provide a few examples of churches that did not consider the potential for distorted communication.

Recently I saw a newspaper advertisement for a church that was hoping to reach the lost. The ad featured a very stern, almost angry-looking pastor, seated in a chair with a Bible in his hand, who stared straight into the camera. The large, bold caption above the picture read: "Come hear Pastor X preach on why most people are going straight to hell." Upon reading the fine print below the photograph, it seems that the intention was to provide a factual message that would answer innocent questions about salvation and damnation. The message that came across from the ad, however, was very emotion evoking.

The church failed to recognize that their communication entered a dimension on which emotion runs deep. Their approach to communicating a basic scriptural truth was to lay out the facts in as bold a manner as possible. Many readers of the ad, however, would interpret the message as a guilt-producing one that placed the church and its people in a holier-than-thou light and characterized the reader as lost and hopeless. That's not great motivation to climb out of bed Sunday morning to hear an angry-looking person rail about damnation.

Churches communicate through more than just their advertising. Take the case of church names and physical facilities. One church that has gained considerable media attention is called "Matthew's Party." It is geared to the baby boom generation and meets on a Saturday night at a racquetball court. Now, I am the last person in the world to chastise a church for attempting to be creative and relevant. This church gains high marks for having a heart to reach people in a nonthreatening environment, and for seeking to be practical and relevant.

However, my informal interaction with people from that area indicates that the church is not taken seriously by many of the people it ought to be attracting. Why? The name removes the church from the realm of the serious and substantive. Someone who is interested in attending a church to grow spiritually or to worship God would be unlikely to select a congregation that describes itself as a party. Although the pastor would disagree that this church suffers from ineffective communication, because he is not open to understanding how the message being received differs from the message being sent, there is a perceived difference between a celebration and a party. Worship can be celebration. In Southern California, however, portraying a gathering as a party conveys an entirely different image. The place chosen for this church service, a public racquetball center, only underscores the dubious sincerity of the intended experience.

Another church was preparing to open its doors for its first service. It had decided to use the name Southwind Church to capitalize on its location close to the ocean and convey a contemporary, peaceful image. Fortunately, in testing the name, the church discovered that many adults in the target audience would have shied away from it because of that name. They interpreted the name very differently than was intended. To the average person, the name sounded like a cult or a church that was theologically adrift. The name was promptly discarded and a more appealing one was chosen.[1]

A small church in the Midwest had used the motto "the friendliest church in town." It's a nice expression, but it, too, carried some negative baggage. First, the motto effectively alienated the church from other Christian churches in the community. The church had failed to think through the consequences of the communication among all of the audiences that would be exposed to the message. Second, the church failed to realize any growth, despite a healthy number of visitors passing through the doors. Why? Because the message promised something the congregation did not deliver. In the secular world, this is known as deceptive advertising. The church can be guilty of it, too, despite the best of intentions.

Even in the worship service, I have seen and heard many unfortunate statements that communicate something entirely different from what was intended. As a common example, think about how a nonbeliever reacts to statements like, "You can be part of our family by joining the church." Does that mean that only card-carrying church members are loved, accepted, or nurtured in that place? Some nonChristians I know have reacted by noting that such statements reinforce their negative perception of the church as a group that seeks to be an exclusive club in which only dues-paying members are welcome. They question the sincerity of our love if we can only attend to our members' needs. Interestingly, the statement may not specifically state that we will ignore those who are not members, but that is the message received. The message was distorted by the receiver, not by the sender, but the sender will bear the unfavorable consequences of that distortion.

When thinking about how you can improve your messages to avoid unintended consequences, be aware of the three primary types of problems that can occur. Sometimes we are at fault for sending the wrong message: one with erroneous content or one sent to the wrong audience. In other cases, the message is distorted because we convey the information improperly or because the receiver misinterprets the message. The examples listed in the preceding paragraphs are examples of such difficulties. Finally, it is possible for the message to be rejected. The person on the receiving end will either ignore the message because it is perceived to have no relevance or intrigue, or the receiver will refute the message.

Advertising as Communications

When we speak of communicating messages about the church to an external public, advertising is the form of communication that usually comes to mind.

Can advertising for churches be effective? *Yes*. Is it usually effective? *No*.

Evaluations of reactions to church advertising clearly indicate that most people believe advertising a church is an appropriate activity. However, when comparing church advertising, as a whole, to advertising from other industries, church ads were rated lower than all other types. People generally felt that church ads were not interesting, memorable, or persuasive.[2]

Strengthen a Weak Message.

Our research suggests that church advertising suffers from three major faults. The first weakness is in the message itself. Look at the print advertising you see in your community for churches. The vast majority of newspaper ads for churches have a picture of the church or pastor, the church's name, the address and telephone number, the times of Sunday services, and the title of the sermon. Now, try to evaluate such an ad objectively. Is it likely to look so interesting that the human eye would gravitate to it? Does it provide information that is so persuasive that a person is likely to change his or her plans in order to visit the church on Sunday? Is the communicated image of the church so strong and favorable that the reader will retain the name of the church and desire further connection with the organization?

Today you will be exposed to about 1,500 commercial messages. We are constantly bombarded by requests urging us to react in a prescribed manner. Many of those are prepared by advertising experts, yet only about two percent of the ads to which we are exposed ever get through our perceptual screening process to penetrate our consciousness. As you look at the typical church print ad, does it stand a chance of breaking through the clutter and arresting your attention? Does it have hope of gripping you with such compelling information that you will change your attitudes or behavior to take advantage of this newfound information?

Few church leaders understand enough about advertising and communications to design a useful ad. Essentially, we are dabbling in a communication form which we know little or nothing about. Yet we squander our limited, precious resources without a second thought and rely on our amateurish approaches to reach our audience.

Advertise at the right frequency.
Besides the problems connected with the message, we are hindered by a problem that advertisers call "frequency and reach." This means we do not advertise frequently enough to accomplish our objectives. It also means we are not reaching enough of the people in our target audience to make any meaningful impact.

For the sake of illustration, let's stick with newspaper advertising as our case in point. In the Los Angeles area, I have watched with interest as computer dealers slug it out for market share. They advertise several times a week. Do they advertise in the business section? Absolutely not! They know enough about their audience to realize that the average buyer is an upscale individual, most likely a male, who is buying the equipment for a small business or for private use. Placing ads in the business or financial section would likely reach men who work for large corporations. Those companies have comparatively little need for computers, and the average reader would not be in a position to make computer purchases anyway. Also, people who read the financial section tend to spend less time reading those pages; they simply look for items of special interest before moving on to other things. So where do the computer retailers place their ads? In the sports section. That is the section their target audience reads consistently and avidly.

Where do we place our ads for church advertising? In most markets, they are relegated to the page or two devoted to religion in the Saturday edition of the newspaper. Think about it. Who will you reach on those pages? The people who are already into religion and most likely have a church home. Think about the timing. Is Saturday the best day for an ad or have readers already made their weekend plans by the time the Saturday newspaper arrives? Certainly, there is much to be questioned about how we target our communications.

Select the right media.
A third concern is our selection of media for communicating our message. Most churches, if they do any advertising whatsoever, place it in the local newspaper and perhaps a display ad in the telephone book.

Do you realize that there are more than twenty-five different advertising media?[3] While only a handful of them have much potential for churches, it is important to think through the different media and how to maximize their impact for the purposes of the church. We should develop a mix of different media to make the most of our opportunities for reaching the market. Reliance on a single medium to reach people is an old-fashioned strategy that reduces our potential influence.

Tips from the professionals.
Advertising professionals offer some useful tips on how to best use advertising for our advantage. Ad agencies understand the advertising process and generally prepare a media plan for their clients. The plan indicates which ads will be used, in which media, and when the advertising will be run. The agencies seek to calculate the financial efficiency of different placement strategies by evaluating how many people in the target market will be reached in relation to the amount of money spent to reach them. It behooves us in the church to operate with equal intelligence as we use the resources God has provided for reaching the community.

Advertising creative teams also recognize that an ad will not perform well unless it says something interesting, indicates how the product is unique or distinctive, and is believable. Once again, we must examine our advertising to determine whether or not we are maximizing our communications in light of what does and does not work today.

It is also critical that we keep in mind a fundamental principle of Christian communication: the audience, not the message, is sovereign.[4] If our advertising is going to stop people in the midst of hectic schedules and cause them to think about what we're saying, our message has to be adapted to the needs of the audience. When we produce advertising that is based on the take-it-or-leave-it proposition, rather than on a sensitivity and response to people's needs, people will invariably reject our message.

Communications for Church Marketing
How does all of this fit in with a marketing perspective for churches? You can recognize that if we do not adequately relate our vision, plans, or intentions, and our heart to other people and organizations, we stand little chance of bringing our dreams to fruition. Without solid communication, we will

be frustrated in our attempt to minister effectively and expand the scope of the church's leadership beyond the existing team.

I recommend that in thinking through your communications needs and approaches, you construct a simple communications plan. It would be a document that indicates who has what responsibilities, which media will be involved, how funds will be allocated for communicating, and so forth. The communications plan is merely an extension of the marketing plan, and might well be incorporated into that plan. The value of taking the time and effort to devise a communications plan is that it will force your church to address how communication will occur to maximize the marketing plans you have prepared. In other words, it is an attempt to reduce the possibility that your marketing operations will be rendered meaningless by unsatisfactory communications.

Having spent this chapter discussing what we say and how we say it, keep in mind that communication is only partially what we say. The most meaningful and credible communication is what we do: Actions do speak louder than words. Thus, while I believe we need to intelligently outline how we use verbal and written communication to move people, we must also realize that when we say one thing and do another, we undermine our ability to minister. By sending a mixed message to people, we send up the red flag in their minds, rendering the remainder of our marketing efforts virtually meaningless. People will not invest time and energy in an organization that is at odds with itself. Our lifestyles and behavior must therefore match what we say we offer and how it will impact people's lives.

NOTES: 1. Based on a research study conducted by the Barna Research Group, Glendale (Calif.), for North Coast Presbyterian Church, Encinitas (Calif.).
2. "The Church Goes Madison Avenue," in *Christian Marketing*

Perspective (Glendale, Calif.: Barna Research Group, July/ August 1986), page 3.

3. For a list of these media, see Philip Kotler and Alan Andreasen, *Strategic Marketing for Non-Profit Organizations* (New York: Prentice-Hall, Inc., 1987), page 506.
4. For a good discussion of the distinctives of communication for the benefit of the church, see James Engel, *Contemporary Christian Communications* (Nashville: Thomas Nelson Publishers, 1979).

10
Church Marketing: A Step, Not a Panacea

If you look at the nonfiction books that sell most briskly these days, the biographies of business leaders are among those that head the list. As I write this chapter, the stories of John Sculley of Apple Computers, Roger Enrico of Pepsi, Debbie Fields of Mrs. Fields' Cookies, David Ogilvy of Ogilvy & Mather, Buck Rogers of IBM, and Akio Morita of Sony are among the best-selling books.

Research tells us that these books, and others before them (like Lee Iococca's book), sell well because the leaders of today's business world are looking for models they can emulate—individuals whose success can be dissected and applied in other situations by people who want to market themselves and their products more effectively. I suppose if I wanted to stretch the point, I could claim that since the Bible is the best-selling book of all time, thousands of people out there must be reading it and absorbing the marketing lessons of Jesus Christ. But even I wouldn't believe that one! However, the idea is sound.

As I mentioned early in the book, I believe we can follow the life of Jesus and glean many tips on how to successfully market the Church. Although our focus is almost always on how Jesus ministered to people—and I am not suggesting that our focus ought to be anything different, for even as we market the Church, our primary responsibility is to share Christ with a lost world—it would be to our advantage to also spend time evaluating how Jesus went about marketing His ministry.

Perhaps the single most important marketing lesson Jesus taught was that marketing is not a one-time event, but a lifestyle. Read the synoptic gospels and marvel at His commitment to His ministry. Read the Gospel of John and be struck by Jesus' sense of timing and His plan—how everything had a time and place, how sensitive He was to the needs of the people He encountered, and how seriously He took the communication of His ministry. Every situation He encountered was seen as an opportunity to reach out and touch someone with His product, that is, with the opportunity to know Him and build an eternal relationship with Him. Clearly, He knew His goals and created opportunities to fulfill people's needs by offering His product, thereby satisfying His goals as well.

Jesus ought to be our model in ministry and in marketing. Just as He did, we have to become so dedicated to, and immersed in, the development of Christianity that it becomes an ingrained part of our everyday behavior. We have to evaluate all situations in light of how we can work with people and situations for the advantage of the Church.

Paul wrote that we are to be ambassadors of Christ. In contemporary language, I interpret that to say that you and I are to be marketing agents of the Church, spreading the good news through all available means and helping build the local church through our marketing efforts.

In evaluating Jesus' ministry, it is also apparent that His work was constantly evolving. He was never satisfied to sit back and rest on His laurels. He was perpetually adapting to new circumstances, each of which brought a new opportunity to reach people. That ability was a function of maintaining a clear, focused perspective. Our goal, too, should be to achieve such a level of sensitivity that we regard every circumstance as a new challenge or opportunity to reach the world.

But as we look at Jesus the marketer, we also have to realize that He paid a price for His marketing activities. His product was not always warmly received. His communication, divinely inspired and perfect as it was, was often misinterpreted. The cost He required for His product was rejected by many. Since His distribution system (the apostles) was inefficient in the beginning, He often had to bear double the burden that would be expected of another marketing executive. So I offer a word of advice and encouragement: If you really believe in what you are doing to market your church, remember that even Jesus faced His share of rejection and His work was successful partially because He was diligent.

Perseverance. Commitment. Faith. These are three indispensable characteristics of a successful church marketer. If we truly believe that Jesus is our only hope, that the Church is His instrument for guiding people and nurturing them to higher levels of spiritual development, and that we have been called by Him to make the Church a reliable source of spiritual truth and righteousness that is accessible to all people, then we must exhibit the depth of that faith by remaining unwavering in our commitment to marketing the Church for His glory.

Practically speaking, this means continuing to implement a marketing plan when people shout insults, claiming that we have turned our backs on the Holy Spirit and are failing to trust God. They may not realize that God has called us to behave intelligently, using the means and resources He has provided to accomplish His ends. Many of our critics will fail to realize that the marketing process itself is neither holy nor unholy; it is how we use and perceive the process, and the fruits of the process, that determine whether or not we have abused it. If we put all our trust in our own marketing abilities, or if our marketing efforts are successful in reaching people for the Church, and we give all the credit to the marketing process rather than to God's blessing on our efforts, only then are our critics correct.

In evaluating whether or not we are marketing effectively, we also have to be wary not to confuse successful marketing with successful ministry. Effective marketing provides the opportunity to minister in a meaningful and significant way. Effective marketing does not mean that the Church is doing all that it has been called to do at a maximum level of quality.

Signs of Success

You probably know a few churches like the one I am about to describe. Perhaps your acquaintance with such bodies remains a concern regarding the acceptability of becoming involved in church marketing.

The church is in the South. Over the years, it has grown to the point where several thousand people attend the worship services every Sunday morning. The preaching is good, but not as good as it used to be. The music is well-rehearsed and biblically solid, but not as crisp as in past years. Why has the church lost its edge? Primarily because the church leaders have become so enamored with numbers that they have neglected their true mission: to reach the hearts of the people who come to the church for nourishment, challenge, and an experience with God. Technique and head counting have gotten in the way of the ministry.

Yes, this church has figured out how to market to its

community. But it has allowed a marketing strategy to over-power the quality of the product. It is forgetting how to minis-ter for the glory of God's Kingdom. It has no desire to cheat God or steal His thunder. The church leaders have simply gotten caught up in the excitement of having the "biggest." Because their judgment has been clouded, they equate being the big-gest with being the best. They have lost sight of their bottom-line goal, which the marketing orientation was designed to help them achieve, of saving souls and edifying believers.

How, then, can your church know if its marketing is effective and on track? Assuming that your marketing plan is geared to creating a church that is growing in numbers, let me suggest a few simple tests.

Growth in numbers.
First, you should experience growth in numbers—the numbers of people who visit your church, join your church, and accept Christ as Savior. Since the purpose of your marketing efforts is to address people's needs, you most likely have either mis-judged people's needs or have not effectively figured out how to address those opportunities for ministry if you are not growing. Likewise, if you are seeing many new faces in the congregation, but few are accepting the Lord, you need to reexamine the strategies you have developed and implemented for guiding people through the spiritual growth process.

Greater involvement.
Second, you should find that as a result of your marketing activities a greater number of people are actively involved in the work of the church. When people catch a vision that is meaningful and exciting, they invariably commit a part of themselves to it. God has prepared every person for such involvement, gifting each individual with talents and capabili-ties that can be used in the marketing campaign. If you have

developed a strong marketing campaign, everyone should be able to find a niche that suits them—one that helps them feel good about making a contribution to the growth of the church.

Excitement.

Third, there should be a sense of excitement about what the church is doing and how it is evolving. When marketing works, it is an exhilarating experience!

How would you have felt to have been part of Ronald Reagan's marketing team that carried him to the presidency in 1980? Think about what it must have been like to be on the marketing team that brought Builder's Emporium, the home improvement chain, back from the brink of bankruptcy to leadership in its industry. Instead of a line of creditors, scholars and journalists wanted to study their work, and investors wanted their share of the pie. How about Disney Studios? Michael Eisner's group of marketing mavins transformed an old-fashioned, moribund, movie studio into the hottest production house in Hollywood. The people in your church can become every bit as excited as these stalwart teams if they catch the vision, receive proper direction, and sense ownership in a ministry that is really going somewhere. Everybody loves a winner!

Sensitivity to ministry.

A fourth indicator of successful marketing in your church is a greater sensitivity to the nature and quality of the church's ministry. By working through the marketing planning process, you will take stock of what the church is doing, how well it is doing it, and what it hopes to accomplish in the future. As a growing team of people becomes involved in the marketing process, and as the congregation becomes increasingly informed about church plans and tactics, members should become more aware of how satisfactorily the church is doing what it is in business to do: minister to people.

Shared responsibility.
A fifth sign that your marketing is successful is when the burden of doing all the work is removed from the back of the pastor. Church marketing is not a one-man show. In the early stages that may be inevitable, but as the church grows and people become excited, more and more individuals will show interest in joining the bandwagon.

A changed atmosphere.
Finally, if the atmosphere at the church changes, it may be due to good marketing. When things start to happen, the entire mood of the church can be radically uplifted. Every once in a while, after you have been implementing your marketing strategies for some time, take a moment to step back and observe what is happening. Can you feel a different aura about the church? Is there a greater sense of purpose, enthusiasm, and joy? Without taking away what rightfully belongs to the Holy Spirit, part of the change in the environment might be attributable to the gains made through the marketing process.

The Importance of Feedback
Regardless of whether the success in your marketing is obvious or not, I cannot overemphasize the importance of developing feedback systems. Unless you are sensitive to what is happening, and are not simply relying on your own limited and possibly biased information and interpretation, your efforts might be wasted. You do not need the world's most sophisticated tracking systems to get a handle on how things are going. But you should have multiple systems in place to give you a comprehensive, reliable perspective on what is happening.

Simple data can be collected regularly and analyzed for trends. For example, you could find out how many people attended the worship service, how many attended the Sunday school classes, how many children were in the nursery, or how many visitors were present. Having such easy-to-collect data can enable you to begin to see the effect your marketing activities have had.

Another key is to track what happens to visitors. Do they return after their first visit? After their second? Do they attend a Sunday school class? How did they learn about the church? What caused them to try your church? Do they eventually join the church? How long does it take them to decide to join? Charting such simple and basic information can help you see patterns in activity that identify how well you are building the kind of church you want.

It is also important to obtain regular feedback from members. This should be done in as nonthreatening and unbiased a manner as possible. Talking informally with members in settings other than the church grounds is helpful, and relying on people other than the pastor to obtain the information is wise. Even such time-worn methods as having a suggestion box can be useful. A more formal approach, such as congregational surveys, can also be invaluable, as long as they are intelligently conducted and not done too frequently (no more than once a year).

It is also advisable to conduct a marketing audit. One simple approach is to identify a team of people that might be qualified to evaluate the church and, then, have them visit the church for several weeks before drawing their conclusions. These judges should be Christians who are familiar with church life and who have had the vision of the church explained to them before their visit. That explanation will enable them to put their observations into an analytic context. The judges should be individuals from other churches because a member of the church cannot be an objective evaluator.

Who could you ask to perform a marketing audit? You might try business professors from a nearby college, graduating eminarians, representatives from your denomination, or marketing consultants who would be willing to assess your progress. The results of their observations should be provided in written form, and should include recommendations of activities that might further improve your church.

Growth Without Compromise

Growth is an indication that something exciting and meaningful is happening. Growth itself can be exciting too. If you are truly seeking growth for the glory of God's Kingdom rather than for yourself, you have to be extremely cautious not to become so numbers crazy that you lose sight of your original purpose.

A church in Southern California began with less than a dozen people attending the first week's service. You cannot find a seat in the sanctuary today, because more than 10,000 people regularly file into the church every Sunday. But the growth of the church occurred as a consequence of spiritual compromise. People who attend that church see a good show, but they don't hear the gospel the way Jesus proclaimed it. Yes, this church is well marketed, but it is marketed for a different purpose than to serve Jesus Christ.

Make no mistake about it: marketing can become so engulfing, so exciting, that it begins to feed on itself. Your job is to master the marketing process, but not to let it master you and your church.

At what point is marketing most likely to lead to compromise in your ministry? From my experience, these are the weak points:

- Getting so carried away with the power of advertising that truth becomes secondary to the number of people reached with the message;
- Becoming so hooked on numerical growth that the preaching of the gospel gets watered down to a

"cheap grace," "name it and claim it," or some other
form of perverted spiritual teaching;
• Changing the vision from one of reaching people for
the spiritual renewal that can happen, to reaching
the greatest number of people so that the church will
be known as the largest or fastest growing church,
regardless of its spiritual life.

If God chooses to bless your marketing efforts, keep in
mind that your success is because of His blessing. Our purpose
is to glorify Him. When we lose the perspective, numbers or no
numbers, we will be worse off than when we started our quest.

Marketing Helps, But Is Not the Only Answer
I wish I could tell you that if your church followed everything
in this book, you would have to build a new, multistory building to handle the overflowing crowd that rushes to your services every Sunday morning to listen to a vibrant, meaningful
message from God's Word. Naturally, that is an unrealistic
expectation. Even if you market your church effectively, your
growth may be modest, rather than explosive. Why? Because
marketing is only one step in the process of building a successful ministry. It is an important step—an often overlooked
step—but it is not the end-all for church growth.

Think about your worship service. Suppose the sermon on
Sunday morning is absolutely superb. Will that cause the
church to grow like wildfire? Not in and of itself, although it
will certainly be a key element to growth. Think of all the other
activities that have to occur in concert with superb preaching.
The music should be passable, if not outstanding. The worship
experience should be of high quality. Parking and seating must
'e available. People must know about the church and be made
're of the amazing sermons flowing from the pulpit. All of
' elements are related and must be working to complement

each other. No single element is adequate to build a church—not even a great marketing plan and its implementation.

Is marketing, then, worth the effort? Yes! You are working with the resources provided by God to enhance your effort toward having a meaningful, growing ministry in people's lives. How can you reject that opportunity?

APPENDIX
Church Growth Resources: Where to Turn for Help

There is no sense reinventing the wheel when it comes to marketing. If your church is like most others, time is of the essence; there are great opportunities to minister to people, opportunities that will be squandered if you wait. Yet, your resources are probably too limited to do everything you would like to do. That means you need to learn what you can from others, take on new challenges, and do your best—all compacted into little time and done on a shoestring budget. It's not an easy task!

Many existing resources can help you better understand the marketing process. This section provides an overview of the potentially most-valuable resources. Some approach marketing differently than I have outlined, and a few arrive at different conclusions. They are included, though, so that you may gain exposure to a diversity of reasonable perspectives toward developing your own unique style and strategies for growing your church.

Books on Church Growth

There are dozens of books about the church growth process. Here are some of the more popular or insightful books in that genre, listed chronologically.

Growing Plans by Lyle Schaller (Abingdon Press, 1983). Deemed the dean of church dynamics, Schaller has written more than thirty books about church organization and development. This volume articulates his advice regarding the steps toward achieving growth.

Strategies for Church Growth by C. Peter Wagner (Regal Books, 1987). Wagner is Donald McGavran's best-known student and colleague. Among the many growth-related books Wagner has written, this is probably most valuable in relation to thinking strategically and practically about reaching more people.

Ten Innovative Churches by Elmer Towns (Regal Books, 1991). Towns studied many churches and chose these as ten of the most interesting and instructive. The book details what makes them tick. He explores the differences in leadership; programming, ministry perspective, and philosophy of the ten congregations. He also attempts to summarize the most instructive principles learned from their experience.

Twelve Keys to an Effective Church by Kennon Callahan (Harper & Row, 1987). A church-management consultant, Callahan outlines a dozen principles that he finds integral to effective church ministry. The book contains both mathematical formulas and theoretical discussions regarding procedures for reinvigorating a church.

Understanding Church Growth by Donald McGavran (Eerdmans, 1990). This is the seminal work by the pioneer in the field. Founder of the Church Growth Movement emanating from Fuller Seminary, McGavran describes the theological and cultural bases of church growth, the role of the pastor and laity, and key growth principles (e.g., homogeneous people).

User Friendly Churches by George Barna (Regal Books, 1991). This is a study of the principles for church ministry employed by some of the fastest-growing Christian churches in the nation. The book identifies and describes more than twenty characteristics that these bodies had in common, although they are different sizes, of different denominational affiliations, and have different ministry goals.

Publications About Marketing

If you are interested in learning more about marketing itself, literally thousands of books have been written about the many aspects: theory, principles, techniques, and case studies. Many are so geared to for-profit enterprise that their value to churches is limited, at best. Listed here are a few books about marketing that present reasonably accessible applications for church leaders who have little or no business training but wish to glean useful marketing concepts or knowledge for ministry. The books are listed in chronological order.

Guerrilla Marketing by Jay Conrad Levinson (Houghton Mifflin, 1985). This may be the best secular book about how to market an organization effectively with limited resources. Practical, simple overview of procedures and concepts for the beginning marketer. Levinson also has two follow-up books that provide additional simple, but valuable insights into marketing activity.

Positioning by Al Ries and Jack Trout (Warner Books, 1986). Although the book is horrendous grammatically (it's written by two advertising executives who butcher the language in an effort to make it user friendly), it conveys crucial marketing concepts in easy fashion. The focus is on positioning: how to place your entity in the most favorable way in the minds of your target audience.

Strategic Marketing for Nonprofit Organizations by

Philip Kotler and Alan Andreasen (Prentice Hall, 1987). This college textbook offers an excellent, comprehensive examination of the multiple facets of marketing an organization when the goal is not simply net profits. The book contains both theory and case studies of applications.

Marketing Your Ministry by John Pearson and Robert Hisrich (Word, Inc., 1990). This is a quick-read, simple treatment of the basic application of marketing thinking to church-based ministries.

Church Marketing by George Barna (Regal Books, 1992). Designed as a follow-up to *Marketing the Church,* this volume walks church leaders through such marketing procedures as designing and implementing research, how to obtain and utilize secondary data, thinking strategically about ministry, creating effective communication vehicles, capturing God's vision for the church's ministry, and developing a comprehensive marketing plan for the ministry. A range of examples are included.

Marketing for Nonmarketers by Houston Elam and Norton Paley (AMACOM, 1992). A very good primer on marketing basics, from concept to product sale. This book gives an overview without getting mired in details.

Conducting Research
A variety of books discuss the how-to's and the why-bother's of research. Perhaps the most readable and practical—each covering a different dimension of the research process—are these three.

Survey Research Handbook by Pamela Alreck and Robert Settle (Irwin Books, 1985). Designed as a college text, this is the most thorough, yet readable book on how to design surveys. The book deals primarily with questionnaire design and sampling.

Focus Groups by Jane Farley Templeton (Probus Publishing, 1987). This is a thorough—sometimes too thorough—guide to conducting focus group research. The author discusses theory, practical techniques, and applications. This book contains more than you need to know about focus groups, but it is helpful in placing the process and techniques in proper perspective.

Beyond Mind Games by Rebecca Piirto (American Demographics Books, 1991). This is the best description yet of psychographics—understanding research related to lifestyles and values. The book discusses many of the cluster research techniques used by churches but rarely understood by church leaders (PRIZM, MicroVision, ACORN, etc.). Useful explanations of an evolving research art.

Understanding People and Society

Every church leader must understand the people group that the church is targeting and the cultural context for the ministry. Several books have provided insights into people's behavior and the social conditions in which people make life decisions. In chronological order, here are some of the best.

Why They Buy by Robert Settle and Pamela Alreck (Wiley & Sons, 1986). A thorough exploration of what motivates people to acquire things. The discussion of psychological and emotional motivations is insightful. The book possesses direct applications for your outreach efforts.

The People's Religion by George Gallup, Jr., and Jim Castelli (Macmillan, 1989). The dean of survey research created a book that brought together an interesting examination of people's religious beliefs and practices based on Gallup studies over the last fifty years.

Dying for Change by Leith Anderson (Bethany House, 1990). Pastor of a church in Minnesota, Anderson has drawn on cultural research and his own experiences to portray a new social reality for churches and ask questions about the new forms the American church must consider if it is to remain accessible for most people.

The Frog in the Kettle by George Barna (Regal Books, 1990). This book offers a look at what the church can expect to encounter by the turn of the decade. Calling church leaders to anticipate change rather than always react to it, the author cites much research toward building an alternative picture of reality for the church—not always pleasing, but generally challenging.

Power Shift by Alvin Toffler (Bantam Books, 1990). The final installment in Toffler's trilogy about change and the future in our culture, this book is the best about coming conditions and how to cope with those transformations. Great insights into human behavior, institutional drag, and cultural realities.

Racing Toward 2001 by Russell Chandler (Zondervan and Harper Collins, 1992). A journalist, Chandler has put together a compilation of research facts and perspectives that place the changing role of religion and Christianity in a useful analytic context. The book includes examples of several churches that are developing adaptive ministry models.

The Barna Report by George Barna (Regal Books, annual). Based on a pair of large, annual surveys conducted by Barna Research, these explore people's changing beliefs, values, lifestyles, and expectations. Each volume provides readers with the survey data tables, as well as commentary on the ministry significance of the latest conditions in which we minister.

Books About People Groups

Research has shown that the most successful churches target a specific group of people and design the ministry to meet their unique needs. Though not excluding anyone, outreach has a focus that enables it to be more effective. Here are a few books focusing on specific people groups that you could target for your church.

Age Wave by Alan Dychtwald (Tarcher Books, 1990). The best discussion of the aging of America and the implications for all aspects of life. As the boomers age, major restructuring of all institutions must occur to accommodate new needs related to aging.

The Baby Boomerang by Doug Murren (Regal Books, 1990). This book explores the baby boomers and how to minister to them effectively. Contains real-life examples along with clear concepts of how to penetrate this large generation.

The Invisible Generation: Baby Busters by George Barna (Barna Research Group, 1992). This book examines the values, lifestyles, religious practices and beliefs, and future expectations of the generation that follows the boomers. Though generally a generation ignored by churches, they represent a key to the future of the church in the United States.

Books About Vision and Leadership

There is little that is more important—or exciting—than grasping God's vision for your ministry. In truth, this is not simply an academic exercise but an act of obedience. To minister effectively and faithfully, we must be seeking to carry out the unique calling God has for each of us. Understanding vision—what it is, how to capture it, and what to do with it—is fundamental to effective leadership.

Leaders by Warren Bennis and Burt Nanus (Harper & Row, 1985). Perhaps the most influential and readable book on leadership, the coauthors provide a fast-reading exploration of what makes a leader effective.

The Seven Habits of Highly Effective People by Stephen Covey (Simon & Schuster, 1989). A well-conceived volume about the key principles that turn an average manager into a powerful leader. These principles transcend mere on-the-job performance; they intrude into the daily fabric of a leader's life.

Developing a Vision for Ministry by Aubrey Malphurs (Baker Book House, 1992). Conceived with church leaders in mind, this book offers a practical guide to understanding how vision fits into the scope of ministry and how to arrive at an understanding of your vision.

The Power of Vision by George Barna (Regal Books, 1992). Based on research among church leaders, this book is geared to describing what vision is, why it's imperative for ministry leaders, how to capture it, attributes of God's vision rather than man's, how vision differs from mission, and how to gain widespread ownership of that vision among the congregation.

Periodicals of Value

With change happening at an alarming pace, trying to remain current means doing more than just reading books. Many periodicals identify the latest and most important trends, techniques, and challenges. Here are a few that you ought to know about.

Advertising Age. The bible of the advertising industry, it offers the most up-to-date view on communications, marketing, and product development. Helpful for understanding the competitive environment of the church.

American Demographics. Probably the best publication for providing a readable and practical understanding of demographic changes and realities. Published monthly, it is not ministry based but has useful insights that can be adapted to your needs.

Brandweek. Formerly *Marketing Week*, this weekly journal provides a marketer's view of the world and how to penetrate an overstimulated and over-saturated consumer with products and services. Like *Advertising Age*, it provides a view of what we're up against in the battle for people's minds and allegiance.

Current Trends and Thoughts. A newsletter that compiles recent national and worldwide events, covering a broad spectrum of activities. Not statistical in nature; essentially a news highlighting service.

Emerging Trends. The monthly newsletter from the Princeton Religious Research Center. Using Gallup Poll data, this six-page publication addresses several issues in each edition, offering the broad view of what's happening in American religious thought and behavior.

The Futurist. Published every other month by the World Future Society, this magazine provides a fascinating glimpse into possible scenarios for the future. It describes new products and services, new ways of perceiving reality, and changes in demographics.

Ministry Currents. A quarterly sixteen-page newsletter from Barna Research outlining the latest in trends affecting the church, along with practical marketing applications. Contains otherwise unreleased data related to church growth and social change.

National and International Religion Report. A biweekly eight-page newsletter briefly identifying key events related to religion that are occurring around the world.

Public Perspective. A compilation of reputable public opinion and behavioral research related to a vast spectrum of themes and issues. Contains limited commentary and many data tables and graphs.

Research Alert. The best newsletter at informing people of recent marketing research studies and their key findings. Although it is not ministry driven, it keeps you current and identifies studies available for purchase.

Other Types of Resources

The primary thrust of several organizations is to help churches be more effective in ministry. Toward that end, they not only produce written materials, but also offer videos, audio tapes, and conduct seminars and consultations. For further information about what they have that might prove to be valuable to you, contact them directly. They are listed alphabetically, with the principle leader indicated in parentheses.

> Alban Institute, Washington, D.C.
> Barna Research Group, Ltd., Glendale, California
> (George Barna)
> Charles E. Fuller Institute, Pasadena, California
> (Carl George)
> Christian Management Association, Diamond Bar, California
> Church Growth, Inc., Monrovia, California (Win Arn)
> Church Growth Institute, Lynchburg, Virginia
> (Elmer Towns)
> Willow Creek Association, Barrington, Illinois
> (Bill Hybels)

Closing Thoughts

In this the Age of Information, there is rarely a lack of information or expertise available to you. The trick is to know what you need, where to find it, and how to use it. When you have specific needs about which you are stumped, network. Ask others for their advice on whom to consult, what to read, which way to turn. Chances are good that you can identify a number of potentially ministry-saving resources through such interaction.

Remember, God wants you to succeed in ministry. He has not placed you in your current circumstance to see you fail.

The resources needed to do the job are available to you. Ask Him and ask His people. And move ahead aggressively in faith that He will bless your efforts to bring glory and honor to Him.

DATE DUE

DEMCO